"This book is not only practical, clear, and concise, it's inspirational! It allows anyone, with any amount of money, to have the tools and THE CHOICE to create more of anything they desire. Truly amazing!"

—Dr Dain Heer, author of *Embodiment-the manual you should have been given when you were born,* and *The joy of being alive*

"This book shows you what else is possible. Chutisa and Steve Bowman have created a book that allows you to choose from a very different place. If you have any desire to create your life as a celebration, then this book is filled with ways to expand you, your money and your life."

—Simone Milasas, CEO/Director, Access Energy Transformation

PROSPERITY
CONSCIOUSNESS

Also by Chutisa and Steven Bowman

Conscious Leadership: The Key to Success, 2005

PROSPERITY CONSCIOUSNESS

Leading Yourself to Money with
Conscious Awareness

CHUTISA AND STEVEN BOWMAN
AUTHORS OF *CONSCIOUS LEADERSHIP*
—THE KEY TO SUCCESS

CONTRIBUTION BY GARY DOUGLAS
AUTHOR OF *MONEY ISN'T THE PROBLEM, YOU
ARE,* AND *MAGIC-YOU ARE IT-BE IT*

iUniverse, Inc.
New York Lincoln Shanghai

Prosperity Consciousness
Leading Yourself to Money with Conscious Awareness

iUniverse books may be ordered through booksellers or by contacting:

iUniverse
2021 Pine Lake Road, Suite 100
Lincoln, NE 68512
www.iuniverse.com
1-800-Authors (1-800-288-4677)

Because of the dynamic nature of the Internet, any Web addresses or links contained in this book may have changed since publication and may no longer be valid.

The views expressed in this work are solely those of the author and do not necessarily reflect the views of the publisher, and the publisher hereby disclaims any responsibility for them.

ISBN: 978-0-595-42596-9 (pbk)
ISBN: 978-0-595-86924-4 (ebk)

Printed in the United States of America

CONTENTS

ACKNOWLEDGMENTS

Our deepest gratitude to Gary Douglas, Dain Heer, and Access Energy for Transformation for showing us how to create a prosperous life and have abundant money with consciousness. Your awareness, creative ideas, and tools were a major contribution to the ease and joy, with which this book was exuberantly transformed into a reality.

We are enormously grateful for Dona Haber, who has worked with conscious awareness as the editor of this book. Thank you, Dona, for the gifts of wisdom, graceful professionalism, and years of experience that you have brought to each page. We could not have finished this book without your professional editorial work.

INTRODUCTION

This book is a gift to everyone who is dedicated to creating a life greater than what they now have and to making a difference in the world. It is a creation of Chutisa Bowman, Steven Bowman, and Gary Douglas, and it is based on the Access Energy for Transformation philosophy of living and our personal and business experience. We aspire to show you how you can lead yourself to money with consciousness and shift any part of your reality that isn't working. This book provides you with tools, inspiration, and transformational processes you can use on your path to success, abundance, and money with consciousness.

You are about to embark on an expedition that will challenge your way of thinking, agitate your points of view, disturb your status quo, awaken your awareness, and expand your possibilities for prosperity. Are you aware that you attract money, wealth, people, events, and circumstances to your life, not by what you do or *have*, but by who you *are*? Are you aware that your consciousness determines whether you will struggle in frustration or live an extraordinary life of abundance and wealth?

You can know everything about investment schemes, financial strategies, real estate investment, and the top secrets of high finance. But if your awareness, or consciousness, concerning money is based on the scarcity paradigm, then you will never have the sense that you have enough money. Moreover, if somehow you are able to acquire a lot of money, you most likely will not appreciate it and, in all probability, will not be able to retain it! The good news is that you can choose to cultivate and expand your consciousness to create success and abundance. This is what we call prosperity consciousness.

Prosperity consciousness is not an extraordinary privilege or a special treat that is only bestowed to some people and not to others. It is a knowable and attainable state of beingness that is available to everyone, if they choose to claim, own, and acknowledge it. We have discovered, over decades of working in this area, that more than anything else, people are held back from being prosperous and successful by their viewpoints about money, prosperity, and abundance. It is not because they were born into a poor family or because they didn't get a college education or because they were disadvantaged to begin with. The lack of prosperity in many people's lives is due to the way they view money and resources. Their viewpoints about money impose severe limitations on the prosperity they can experience. With the points of view they have adopted, they create for themselves a scarcity paradigm.

Prosperity consciousness is not just about possessions and money. It is about a joyful expression of life, a sense of expansiveness, a joy of being, and a sense of abundance in all things. The extraordinary tools, practices, insights, and inspirations contained in *Prosperity Consciousness-Leading Yourself to Money with Conscious Awareness* will facilitate expansion of your prosperity consciousness and set in motion a whole new way of being and living with awareness. You will begin to perceive, know, be, and receive the truth that prosperity and abundance have nothing to do with what you are *doing* and *having*. It has everything to do with what you are *being*. The tools and practices that this book offers will continue to assist you in expanding your consciousness and letting go of your limitations long after you stop reading.

If you are ready to experience unbridled joy, exuberant expression, and the abundance of life, regardless of its challenges, all you have to do is choose to make consciousness the guiding principle in everything you do. The inspirations and transformations you will receive from following the practices in this book will facilitate a wave of change in your financial state and in your life. These will, in turn, affect many other areas of your reality and the world at large. Each time that you choose to expand your consciousness, you change this world into a place in which people can live with total awareness, unbridled joy, and infinite abundance. Not just you, but every other being in this world, are affected by the choices you make.

The writing of this book has been a joyful and expansive experience, and we trust that you will find something herein that relates to your own personal situation. We invite you to stop looking for something to *do* and *have* and to open yourself to perceiving, knowing, being, and receiving the infinite possibilities and what it would take for you to truly *be*. We invite you to get in touch with who you really are and to bring into being the prosperity consciousness that is inherent in you.

MONEY AND CONSCIOUSNESS

In this chapter, Steve explores four areas:

- *Consciousness—the key to generating true wealth and abundance*

- *The scarcity paradigm vs. prosperity consciousness*

- *The myth of "working hard"*

- *Tools you can use to free yourself from limiting beliefs about money*

Have you ever wondered why some people live in poverty and some in enormous wealth? Why some people seem to generate money easily, while others seem destined for a life of financial lack?

We have discovered that people's ability to generate wealth has nothing to do with education, intelligence, work habits, luck, investment know-how, or choice of jobs. The secret is consciousness.

Over the years, my wife Chutisa and I have had many opportunities to work with a number of influential, successful, and resource-rich people. We are frequently amazed by how many of these powerful people struggle to find solutions to what they think of as their money problems. It's obvious that they struggle not because of the actual conditions and circumstances of their lives but because of their lack of awareness, personal perspectives, and dysfunctional relationships with money.

Now, I am the first to admit that Chutisa and I have had plenty of money dilemmas ourselves. We used to fret and torture ourselves when we experienced financial glitches. Like many others, we were buying into these mistaken perceptions:

- I need more money to achieve financial independence.

- I have to work hard to become wealthy and successful.

- I need to put money aside for a rainy day.

- I have to save money for retirement.

We used to think that having great jobs with big companies would put us on the path to financial freedom and success. We thought that successful careers would turn us into wealthy people. And for quite some time, we attempted to create our lives based on these lies, which ultimately created limitations that did not allow us to expand into what is truly possible. The more successful Chutisa and I became, the busier and more tied to our jobs we were.

We were safe, secure, rational, steady, predictable, established, and sensible. We were striving to maintain our financial freedom and the status quo, and we succeeded. This is the lifestyle most people aspire to attain in this reality.

So, what's wrong with that? you may ask.

Nothing! This lifestyle is okay if you are satisfied with being mediocre, run-of-the-mill, and ordinary. There is nothing right, wrong, good, or bad here. This is not a judgment. If this is enough for you, then read no further.

However, Chutisa and I chose to destroy and uncreate all the decisions, judgments, and lies that would not allow us to expand our lives and become truly abundant. This book is about the ideas, processes, and philosophy of life that has enabled us to realize our dreams of prosperity and abundance.

We discovered that the experience of abundance and prosperity is determined by what goes on inside us far more than what goes on around us. We found that when we choose to share our generosity of spirit with those whose lives we touch, then everything we require comes to us with ease, without our even doing anything to obtain it.

We learned that true abundance has nothing to do with what we *have*. It has everything to do with whom we choose to *be*.

We are delighted to share what it took for us to lead ourselves to money with consciousness, utilizing Access Energy for Transformation tools. We do not expect anyone to copy our path, but we do want to share our experience and the tools we used. We encourage you to find your own path to prosperity consciousness.

◆　　　◆　　　◆

Setting the Scene

First, let me set the scene for you.

I grew up in what is typically described as a broken home. My mother left her abusive husband when I was seven years old (my brother was five, and my sister was three). We traveled throughout Australia, always one step ahead of my father. My mother took various jobs to create income for the family, and, while there was always enough to eat and a place to stay, we lived with an underlying fear of "not enough." Members of my family had always worked hard for their money. As a result, I equated working hard with making money. I had no idea that my beliefs could not have been further from the truth.

Chutisa, on the other hand, comes from a wealthy and aristocratic family from Bangkok, Thailand. Her grandfather was a prominent chief justice. She grew up with personal maids and was lovingly pampered by her mother and grandparents. Chutisa was sent off to Australia to study at the age of fourteen.

We met at a country picnic in a little Australian town called Yea when I was eighteen and Chutisa was seventeen. I was in my last year of a scholarship as a boarder at one of Australia's most prestigious private schools. Chutisa was in her second-to-last year of school. We fell in love and got married after we graduated from university. We immediately got great jobs and started our lives together. I was a university lecturer in communication disorders. Chutisa was a fashion model and a high-fashion designer.

In the early 1980s, I was granted a small scholarship to study for a master's degree at George Washington University in Washington DC. We decided to go to the United States for two years to further my education. We gave up our jobs and careers and landed in the United States with our savings and a small amount of money from the scholarship. These funds had to last two years. We had no jobs to return to. The experience of living on a subsistence income during this time period highlighted our issues associated with a scarcity mindset and began our journey to prosperity consciousness.

When we chose to live in the United States under these circumstances, we never once believed that we couldn't do it. In fact, we created even more extreme circumstances for ourselves. I chose to undertake a second master's degree program at the same time. We had to tighten our belts even more, to the extent that we routinely ate one-dollar frozen TV dinners for two years as I studied. Chutisa graciously let go of her successful modeling career, her flourishing fashion design career, and her comfortable life in Australia to be with me in the United States. She created each new day as an adventure without any complaining. We lived for two years on gratitude and trust for each other.

Most people we knew considered our decision to live at a subsistence level in the United States as major risk taking. However, we never considered ourselves to be taking a risk. Instead, we perceived our choice as an adventure and an unbounded opportunity. We were living our lives in each moment as though it was impossible to fail.

Chutisa has great fashion design expertise. While I studied, she created and produced amazing one-of-a-kind Australiana fashion knitwear, and she aimed to sell her creations to anyone who could see their value. One day, we took the train into New York City with twelve of her completed one-off designs. We walked the streets of New York with absolutely no inkling of who to see or how to start. We asked questions of the buyers at some of the largest department stores and exclusive boutiques and were eventually referred to one of New York's most respected fashion agents. He fell in love with Chutisa's work and subsequently promoted her knitwear throughout North America and Europe. This created a good income stream, which we used to supplement our savings and my meager scholarship. We had to watch every cent, though, as this was our only source of income while I was studying.

These two years of living on a bare minimum spawned many scarcity points of view. We bought into the lie that we "didn't have enough money." We decided that we "had to work hard for money" and then created our lives based on that lie. At the same time, this experience also set in motion our gratitude and trust for the universe and highlighted many of our underlying beliefs about our capabilities to succeed.

One of our major positive underlying beliefs has been that the universe is an abundant place. We believed there are truly infinite possibilities. We went to the United States, believing that we would make it but with no idea of how. The prospect of not making it was never a possibility. It was stressful at times, when the bank balance was down to a few hundred dollars, but we knew that money would be coming in—we just didn't know where it would come from.

The second belief, one that limited us, was my idea that I had to work hard to create money. One of my greatest fears was that I would be perceived as lazy. I had to be seen as "busy." This belief was responsible for my strange habit of making work when none was needed. I held on to this old "busy" habit even when I was CEO of some of Australia's most prestigious organizations.

Many years later, after Chutisa and I had discovered the Access Energy for Transformation philosophy, we became aware that we were functioning in a scarcity paradigm. We began to explore what it would take for us to get out of our scarcity mindset and into prosperity consciousness. Through our explorations, we discovered that prosperity consciousness is a matter of choice. If you choose to be prosperous and to be prosperity conscious, then you can be. If you choose not to be prosperity conscious and if you cling to the scarcity paradigm, then you create your life based on that framework. It's your choice!

◆   ◆   ◆

Transforming Your Relationship with Money

Our relationship with money began to transform as soon as we discovered Access Energy for Transformation and began to use its tools and practice its philosophy of living. Throughout this book, we will share our experiences and viewpoints, as well as tools and practices you can use to facilitate expansion of your consciousness around money. We hope these viewpoints, tools, and practices will awaken you to the infinite possibilities you can choose, to lead yourself to money with consciousness.

The aim of *Prosperity Consciousness-Leading Yourself to Money with Conscious Awareness* is to help you awaken and unleash the power of consciousness over money. Along the way, we will explore how and why people diminish their prosperity consciousness, so that you can understand, and then destroy and uncreate, the lies that keep you trapped in a scarcity paradigm. We hope that you will use this book to create a far-reaching transformation in all parts of your life.

This book has nothing to do with how to get rich quick. It doesn't teach you how to invest in property or the stock market. In truth, we would like to encourage you to stop falling for get-rich-quick and anticonscious moneymaking schemes that you hope will put you out of your financial misery.

If you have an anticonscious relationship with money now, you will continue to have the same anticonscious relationship with money no matter how much money you have. Even if you acquire large amounts of money, your dysfunctional relationship with money will continue. It will simply occur at a higher level. Your consciousness always determines your conditions and circumstances. Unless your prosperity consciousness expands, your relationship with money will remain the same. You will continue to have the same degree of limitation and the same degree of financial mess. If you don't transform your consciousness around money, then when you receive more money, your financial mess will simply grow in proportion to the amount you receive.

◆   ◆   ◆

Expanding Your Consciousness around Money

So, where did Chutisa and I begin when we chose to expand our consciousness around money? First and foremost, we began to examine our own relationship with money.

We became aware that each of us had a very specific, yet mostly unexamined and absolutely unconscious relationship with money, which had created and shaped our individual experiences of life. We discovered that we had points of view that were founded in scarcity and limitation. We had to destroy and uncreate those views if we wanted to experience greater wealth and abundance in our lives.

Even though both of us had been doing extremely well in the arena of career achievement and money attainment, we often felt a niggling sense of uneasiness that we would never have as much as we needed to maintain our lifestyle. In reality, the amount of money we had was never the problem. Our angst about money was not a true reflection of how things really were. It was a mindset we had created.

We often experienced the incongruity between the way we imagined life should be and the way we were living it. We were functioning under a self-imposed pressure to earn more, acquire more, invest more, save more, have more, and be more. We were surprised to find that our uneasiness about money did not go away even when we tripled our income (which had already been in six figures). This was truly strange to us. We had expected that such a large increase in our income would make us feel much more prosperous—but it didn't.

We became aware that unless we were willing to change from scarcity consciousness to prosperity consciousness, it was going to be business as usual, regardless of how much money we had. We recognized that even if we were able to generate money with ease, our consciousness would always determine our experience. Unless our consciousness concerning money changed, no matter how much money we created, our experience would remain the same.

◆   ◆   ◆

Shifting the Focus from Scarcity to Prosperity

Chutisa and I began to look at the unconscious conditioning that had trapped us in this cycle of confusion, dissatisfaction, and an endless chase for more. We noticed that we had made money the goal. We had made it a need. We noticed that we would often think things like "if I only had more money" or "money will make me happy and secure." None of this was real.

Looking at our unconscious conditioning was not about sitting in judgment of ourselves. It was about becoming aware of how we had created our reality. We realized that if we could become aware of what we had chosen to create our reality without judging ourselves, we could have freedom, but as long as we had judgment, we had no freedom. This is because if we blame and judge ourselves, then we contract our awareness. Whenever we go into judgment about anything, whether it is a positive judgment or a negative judgment, then we cut off our capacity to receive beyond that judgment. Every judgment we make stops us from perceiving and receiving anything that doesn't match that judgment. However, if we function from the place of no judgment, then we can receive the entirety of the world.

We stopped looking at the wrongness of our financial situation and started asking questions.

What's right about this that we're not getting?

This question allowed us to unlock possibilities for change in our lives.

We became aware that whenever we experienced our lives as a limitation, there had to be something that we were unwilling to perceive, know, be, and receive. We began to ask ourselves this:

What must I perceive, know, be, and receive that would allow me total clarity and ease with money, wealth, prosperity, and abundance?

This question started to unlock the places in our financial life where "we" were not showing up—the places where we were not being conscious. We became willing to look at all our limiting decisions, fears, beliefs, and concerns without judging ourselves for any of them. By putting our entire "financial sob story" out in front of us, we got to see it, and eventually become free of it.

◆   ◆   ◆

Taking a Leadership Role in Our Lives

For Chutisa and me, the key to transforming our consciousness around money was to take a leadership role in our lives. We began to claim, own, and acknowledge that money in itself could not make us happy, secure, or powerful. However, we saw that money could provide opportunities for independence. It could result in the means to facilitate good· for ourselves and others. We chose to become the leaders of our own lives and the creators of our own realities. We decided to take complete responsibility for all that occurred in our lives.

We began to expand our abilities to receive everything with gratitude and without judgment. Furthermore, we also cultivated our abilities to perceive and receive ourselves differently. We chose to create our lives as a celebration instead of as the obligation, work, trauma, drama, upset, and intrigue it had tended to be previously.

◆   ◆   ◆

Creating Our Lives as a Celebration

We now remind ourselves every day to make our lives a celebration. Every morning we say this:

Just for today, my life will be a celebration.

One of the ways I most decidedly was *not* celebrating my life was in the area of the clothes I wore. I used to dislike spending money on clothes for myself, as I believed it was extravagant and unnecessary. I would wear dark suits, white shirts, conservative ties, and inexpensive black shoes. I didn't realize that I had a fixed point of view about not wanting to waste money on clothes—but that's what it was. This fixed point of view got destroyed and uncreated one day when I went shopping in Sydney, Australia, with Gary Douglas and Dain Heer from Access Energy. We went into an exclusive shoe store and Gary suggested that I try on a pair of shoes that caught my eye. I fell in love with the shoes instantaneously and decided to buy them. However, when I went to pay for them, and the sales assistant told me that they were $600, I freaked out. Gary asked me a few questions regarding my unwillingness to create my life as a celebration. This totally broke down my fixed point of view.

I felt the wheels starting to turn in my head after I heard Gary say, "Life needs to be a celebration. If you aren't celebrating your life, you're not living." I was able to see how I had not been creating my life as a celebration in terms of the clothes I wore. From that day forward, I have been buying nice clothes. No more cheap shoes, lackluster suits, and dreary ties. I now have nice designer suits and shirts that are an orgasmic experience to wear. This is one of the many ways I now create my life as a celebration.

In order to create our lives as celebration, Chutisa and I have shifted our focus from scarcity consciousness to prosperity consciousness. We do this by asking for the greatness of us to show up. We ask for the joy and the celebration of our lives. We don't just ask for money, as that would be severely limiting. Money doesn't have anything to do with the greatness of our lives. We do! Since we have been asking for the greatness of our lives and for our lives to be a celebration, new possibilities have been showing up more and more often.

Since we have focused our consciousness toward prosperity, we have attracted immense sums of money to ourselves, and we have truly enjoyed that money. We have experienced firsthand that when we change our focus, we change our financial situation instantaneously.

A client of ours, the CEO of a large not-for-profit organization in South Australia, wrote to us recently stating that after she worked with us and shifted her focus to prosperity consciousness, her organization tapped into an abundance of funding that has nearly doubled their revenue in six months. She wrote us a note:

> The scarcity of funds (now an old thought process) has been replaced by abundance. I now know there is an abundance of funding out there. Since April, we have received a number of unexpected project offers, donations, and bequests. Not only is there abundance in terms of financial benefits, but media coverage and volunteer hours have also increased. As you say, "How does it get any better than this?"

◆   ◆   ◆

Are You Functioning in the Scarcity Paradigm?

To embrace prosperity consciousness, you have to step up and become more than what you have been willing to be. Are you willing to step out of the scarcity paradigm and become the outstanding, glorious, and magnificent being you truly are?

Everything that you think you cannot be greater than—will you destroy and uncreate it please?

When the scarcity frame of mind is deeply entrenched into the way you view yourself and the world around you, it can sabotage your efforts to create wealth. However, if you become aware of the thoughts, feelings, and emotions that you have about money in your everyday life, then you can recognize—and transform—your scarcity mindset.

◆   ◆   ◆

Practical Process: Check off any of the following that you identify with:

• You find yourself going through the day saying, "There isn't enough of this," and "I don't have enough of that."

• Your judgments, outlook, and viewpoints are governed by the fear of not having enough money.

• Money is the number one cause of your stress. "I don't have money" is a thread that runs through your thoughts, feelings, and emotions.

• You stay in a career that you hate for fear of not being able to get another job.

• You spend your days doing work you don't really want to do, just to make more money.

• You have abandoned your dreams and are fearful of taking even the slightest chance with your money.

• You are fearful of losing what you have.

• You are driven in an endless and unfulfilling pursuit of more money, resources, and assets.

• It is difficult for you to share recognition and credit, power, or profit, even with those who assisted you to achieve this outcome.

- You have a hard time being genuinely happy for the success of other people.

- Money causes fighting, struggle, hostility, resentment, and unhappiness in your life.

If you check off even one of these statements, then you are under the spell of a scarcity mindset. Even one of the above outlooks, deeply ingrained within your psyche, is enough to interfere with your efforts to become wealthy and successful.

◆   ◆   ◆

Tools You Can Use to Free Yourself from Limiting Beliefs about Money

Examine your relationship with money.
Discover these things:

- Become aware of your points of view that are founded in scarcity and limitation.

- Discover your limiting beliefs and perspectives about money.

- Become aware of your unconscious conditioning about money—without judging yourself.

- Look at your limiting decisions, fears, and concerns about money.

- Put your "financial sob story" out in front of yourself.

Destroy and uncreate the decisions, judgments, and lies that do not allow you to expand your life and become abundant.
Say to yourself:

- All the decisions, judgments, and lies that do not allow me to expand my life and become abundant, I now destroy and uncreate them totally.

Stop looking at the wrongness of your financial situation and start asking questions.
Ask these questions:

- What's right about this that I'm not getting?

- What must I perceive, know, be, and receive that would allow me total clarity and ease with money, wealth, prosperity, and abundance?

Take a leadership role in your life.
Do these things:

- Claim, own, and acknowledge that money cannot make you happy, secure, or powerful.

- Become the leader of your life and the creator of your own reality.

- Take responsibility for everything that occurs in your life.

Create your life as a celebration.
Do and say these things:

- Every morning, say: "Just for today, my life will be a celebration."

- Make all aspects of your life into a celebration.

- Every day, ask for the greatness of you to show up.

Step out of the scarcity paradigm and become the glorious and magnificent being you truly are.

MONEY IS NOT THE PROBLEM: THE PROBLEM IS OUR UNWILLINGNESS TO RECEIVE

Chutisa discusses the following areas in this chapter:

- *Receiving—how much you are willing to receive*

- *Receiving the greatness of who you truly are*

- *The art of receiving everything without judgment*

- *Tools to enhance your ability to receive money—and everything else*

Money is actually easy to attract. There is an abundance of money and resources—a never-ending supply. It is only unwillingness to receive that makes these things hard to obtain.

We have learned from discussions we have had with clients, colleagues, and workshop participants from around the world that many people have wounds and negative beliefs about money. The wounds and the beliefs have different story lines, but their effects and consequences are always the same: they prevent money from flowing effortlessly through your life. We have discovered that money is never the problem. The problem is your unwillingness to receive, which is a by-product of the way you think about money or about yourself.

◆　　◆　　◆

Becoming Willing to Receive

Steve and I finally came to understand the source of our own and of most people's money problems, during a conversation we had with Gary Douglas, the founder of Access Energy for Transformation. Gary said something that helped us to understand our own state of affairs around money:

> Receiving is the problem—and you are the solution. The issue is not money. The problem is that you are not willing to receive you into your life. The main thing you are unwilling to receive is the greatness of you.

Hmm. Unwillingness to receive the greatness of me is the problem? I was intrigued. Gary suggested that I ask myself and the universe a question:

So, what's it going to take for me to be able to receive the greatness of me?

We were inspired by Gary's statement, that what we were willing to receive determines the amount of money we can have in our lives. He said it was essential to look at what we were unwilling to receive, because this determines the amount of money we are willing to have. We saw that the willingness to receive everything is essential if we desire to create wealth. It is also indispensable if we wish to keep the wealth.

Steve and I realized that we were the only ones who knew what was stopping us. We would only be able to get to the truth of the issue once we acknowledged that receiving is the problem—and we are the solution. We asked ourselves a question:

What am I unwilling to receive about me that, if I were willing, would allow me to have the totality of me?

Then we began to look at what we were unwilling to receive in general. We discovered that we were blocking ourselves from receiving money in the same ways that we were blocking ourselves from receiving many other things in our lives and our work.

◆   ◆   ◆

Receiving the Greatness of You

Becoming aware of what we were unwilling to receive about ourselves was a new frontier for Steve and me. Gary said to us:

> The main thing you are unwilling to receive is the greatness of you. If you are willing to receive the uniqueness and the greatness of you and willing to

allow the world and everyone to see the uniqueness and the greatness of you, the world will then gift to you what you truly deserve.

I asked him, "What would it take for that to happen?"

Gary answered, "Honey, you have to have a willingness to perceive and receive yourself differently. This is the beginning of creating what you truly desire in your life. That's the place where you have to begin."

As I thought about it, I got insight into how I was unwilling to receive the uniqueness and the greatness of me. Not only was I unwilling to receive my greatness; I was actually rejecting, negating, and denying my uniqueness. I didn't want to be different or stand out from the crowd. I was doing everything possible to hide my power. I assumed it was virtuous to be modest, humble, and understated. I thought that the only other alternative was to be obnoxious and full of myself.

I had misidentified and misapplied the notion of humility and modesty. I had been taught during my early years to avoid being conceited, boastful, and self-serving. I was conditioned to turn away from self-acknowledgement and avoid talking about my achievements. I thought it was a good thing to be unassuming and modest about my talents and abilities.

After I talked with Gary, I began to ask myself this question:

What am I unwilling to receive about the greatness of me?

At first, I felt I was being kind of naughty, immodest, and self-centered. Gary and Steve told me to get over myself. This broke down the idea that I needed to conceal my power. My reaction was, "You mean it's not arrogant to receive the greatness of me? Could I really do that without appearing audacious and conceited?" I had utterly bought into the lie that there would be negative consequences if I let myself be seen as confident, glorious, and magnificent.

I had suppressed my confidence and potency, because I thought it was improper, obnoxious, and conceited to be powerful. I had bought these lies and limitations as I was growing up, and then I tried to create my life based on them. I was constantly hiding my power and keeping my talents and gifts hidden from others and from myself.

Once I became aware of what I was unwilling to receive about myself, I was able to stop pretending that I was weak, pale, and uninteresting. I saw that for me to have something glorious and magnificent in my life, I had to develop a more conscious attitude toward my body and myself. I had to be willing to receive myself in totality without judgment. I had to be willing to claim, own, and be everything that I am. I had to be as unconventional, weird, wacky, and outrageous as I truly am—no matter how uncomfortable that might be at first. I had to stop equivocating and choose *me*, no matter what.

The place where I had to start was the willingness to perceive and receive myself differently. I had to stop stifling and suppressing my talents and abilities. Suppression was the way I used to manipulate and control myself. Freedom began with the willingness to receive the greatness of who I truly am—not just to wishfully think about it, but to actually experience it. I had to truly live who I am, right here, right now, instead of thinking about who I am as something outside of me, something that I had to manage, or something that I would like to do in the future.

When I started receiving the greatness of who I truly am, then everything in my life started to transform—including my financial situation. Since then, I have had an array of extraordinary experiences (and have received money), which have further transformed my view of myself and of my potential.

Has anything like this happened to you? How many times have you refused to receive the greatness of who you truly are because you thought that it was improper or because you did not want to be ridiculed? How much more could you have—if you were willing to receive the greatness of who you truly are?

Acknowledge your unwillingness to receive the greatness of who you truly are and all of the talents, abilities, and awareness that you previously decided you couldn't have. Will you now claim and own them and destroy and uncreate everything that doesn't allow them to exist?

One word of warning. If you choose to practice receiving the greatness of who you truly are, you have to be willing to be seen for who you really are. You have to be willing to receive anything from anybody. You have to be willing to receive compliments, accolades, and admiration, as well as criticism, disapproval, and ridicule. You don't have to buy the responses as real; you just have to be willing to receive it all, without judging yourself or others.

◆   ◆   ◆

What We Have Decided That We Can't Receive Limits What We Can Have

Steve and I have made the willingness to receive everything without judgment the guiding principle in our lives. We practice it in our way of being with one another and in our Board and leadership consulting business. If we are experiencing a limitation or difficulty in our lives, whether it has to do with work, family, relationships with clients, business dealings, or even sex and our interactions with each other, we know that there has to be something that we are not willing to receive.

One of the great insights I've had using Access tools is that in order to create any kind of limitation, I realize that I have to cut off my receiving. It is only what I have decided I cannot receive that limits what I can have in life. We have learned that if anything in our lives is not working, it is because we are unwilling to perceive, know, be, or receive something. When we notice that we feel limited, we make it a practice to become more receptive and vigilant. We catch ourselves in the act of resisting or reacting to something and ask ourselves this question:

What am I unwilling to receive here?

In practicing this, we discovered that there was not any one particular point of view, theme, or subject that we were unwilling to receive. It was a myriad of things.

Asking ourselves, "What am I unwilling to receive here?" has allowed us to become more aware of our fixed points of view about our reality and how wealth can be created.

Being open and willing to receive everything with gratitude and without judgment has allowed us to expand our awareness and ability and to access infinite possibilities beyond our previous experience. We've been able to create a highly successful business, as well as new seminars and products, which in turn have created expansion of consciousness for the business world, more clients, and more money for us. But more importantly, we have learned to navigate the world with ease, joy, and an exuberant expression of life. How does it get any better than this? What else is possible?

◆   ◆   ◆

Be Willing to Receive Everything and to Lose Everything

Steve and I have noticed that when we are willing to receive everything and also willing to lose everything, then we expand our capacity to overcome the inevitable obstacles and see things through. The willingness to receive everything without judgment is an art. Its skilled practice takes a great deal of discipline, immense dedication, and powerful determination. We have found that when we are willing to receive everything, we have the benefit of enjoying everything as it is. There is no need to alter or change anything.

We advocate a lifelong exploration of the willingness to receive everything without judgment. This practice requires us to live with total awareness. We discovered that in order to stick with this practice, we have had to do three things:

1. Develop the discipline to notice the times when we refuse to receive.

2. Build the dedication to persevere until greater awareness becomes embedded.

3. Discover within ourselves the strong determination for a conscious way of being.

We have had to step up and become more than what we had been willing to be in the past. This has required the willingness to be more in every respect. We had to stop refusing to be who and what we truly are. We have had to be willing to put ourselves out there in a way we were not willing to before. We have had to be willing to be controversial and to stir the pot. We have had to defy, defeat, and destroy those old, erroneous definitions of ourselves, of each other, and of our business.

Once we made a demand of ourselves to receive the greatness of us, then our business started to expand and thrive more than we could have imagined. We created more clients, more products, more services, more opportunities, and more income. After we made the willingness to receive everything without judgment the guiding philosophy in our lives, our levels of perception, clarity, and insight took gigantic leaps forward. The willingness to receive everything without judgment is the dynamic power that gives us the audacity, confidence, strength, and courage to do what we want with our lives, to see things through, and to overcome the inevitable obstacles.

◆   ◆   ◆

Receiving Everything No Matter What It Looks Like

As soon as we chose to practice the willingness to receive everything, we became willing to be more unconventional and controversial in our work. We talked about notions, concepts and practices that were not often heard about in Boardrooms or senior executive teams. Our business started to expand exponentially, because we were willing to *be* more. We were willing to do things that shifted other people's thinking. We were willing to receive everything, including judgment and criticism, no matter what it looked like. Soon we became leaders and pacesetters on the inspirational and leadership-conference trail, and in great demand for internal workshops with Boards and Directors.

Since Steve has become willing to put himself out there in a way that he was not willing to before, he has been invited to provide keynote presentations to conferences on topics that other speakers feel are too controversial. He now willingly speaks about subjects such as consciousness in corporate strategy setting and Board governance. When he presents to large gatherings at conferences, there are often in excess of six hundred people in the audience. Many of them are not able to receive his message about consciousness and awareness. Since Steve is able to maintain the space of receiving everything, even rejection and criticism, he never gets nervous. He is able to facilitate expansion of consciousness, even for people who are not willing to receive him. He leaves his audiences inspired with practical, conscious leadership tools and tips they can apply at work, at home, and in their communities. Even if some people are unable to accept the message, they still go away with interesting anecdotes and techniques.

Something profound and transformational has happened to Steve as a keynote speaker. Since he has chosen to be willing to receive everything, he has developed greater insight and a clarity of inner vision that he had never had before. He has repeatedly been invited to facilitate workshops that assist senior executives, board members, and leadership teams to become more conscious and to lead with awareness.

We are now willing to be daring and audacious. We speak out on contentious subjects. Because we are willing to receive everything without judgment, business people from all over the world are showing up and inviting us to work with them. How does it get any better than this? What else is possible?

◆   ◆   ◆

What Are You Unwilling to Receive?

Look at what you are unwilling to receive. In truth, if anything in your life is not working, it's because there's something you are unwilling to receive. You may even discover that you're unwilling to receive money!

When we coach people to shift out of their scarcity paradigm into prosperity consciousness, one thing we notice time after time is that their ability to create unlimited amounts of money is conditioned by two factors: the point of view they have about money and a willingness to receive it. We have discovered that the amount of money a person has created in his or her life is in proportion to the willingness or unwillingness to receive it. Said another way, people's willingness to receive money is conditioned by the point of view they have about how money can flow into their lives.

Our clients' ability to receive and create money resides only in the points of view that they have bought as true. The common viewpoint many of our clients have about money is "it is not good to have too much of, and it is not a good thing to receive from others." This viewpoint expresses an unwillingness to receive—from anywhere. Very often people's unwillingness to receive directs the course of their behavior and actions. What they constantly focus on plays a key role in facilitating what, when, where, why, and how money can show up in their physical world.

Practical Process: An important step in cultivating the willingness to receive everything without judgment is developing the willingness to claim and own the capacity to receive, even though you may have no idea what that means or what will be coming to you. A key part of being willing to receive everything is to stop resisting and reacting to any interaction you or anyone else has. When you catch yourself resisting and reacting, ask yourself the following questions:

- What am I unwilling to receive here?

- What ideas or viewpoints have I created that are stopping me from receiving? (These ideas and viewpoints may seem meaningful, significant, or even sacred to you. It may be challenging for you to actually look at them.)

- What would it be like to receive from everybody without judgment?

- What would it be like to receive from everybody without any point of view? (Having a point of view can be a judgement and largely automatic and unconscious)

◆   ◆   ◆

Judgment

The thing that most limited my capacity to receive was judgment. I noticed that whenever I went into judgment about anything, whether it was a positive judgment or a negative judgment, I stopped myself from receiving anything that didn't match that judgment. I discovered that every judgment I had about what money meant to me created parameters around what I could receive. The most limited and absurd judgment I had about money was "it's taboo to talk about money."

I used to see money as part of something I did not understand. I was brought up to believe that discussing money was offensive and in bad taste. I had bought an erroneous point of view that money was a personal subject that shouldn't be discussed and certainly shouldn't be taught or talked about in public. I used to feel embarrassed, frustrated, and uncomfortable when I had to talk about wealth and money. From the moment I chose the path of conscious prosperity, I knew that when I resisted thinking or talking about money, then I was declaring to the universe my unwillingness to receive it.

Here's the bottom line: When I avoided talking about money, or even thinking about it, I was creating barriers to receiving it. My reluctance and resistance were really a receiving issue. Not only that, but it took a huge amount of energy to keep my judgments about money in place. Until I was able to feel good about having money—and plenty of it—I would not be able to receive it.

Once I recognized that, I asked myself two questions:

- **What do I want?**

- **What feels best?**

I realized that I had to choose to be greater than I had been willing to be. I made a demand of myself. I chose to stop putting up barriers to receiving money and to claim and own my ability to talk about money with ease. That decision started the process of becoming excited and wholehearted about seeing the value of me, my life, and my work. I chose to be elated about the way our clients and potential clients could benefit from our services and products.

Practical Process: You are the only one who knows what is stopping you from receiving money. You can use the questions below to help discover the points of view that are preventing you from receiving unlimited amounts of money.

- What am I absolutely unwilling to receive that, if I were willing, would manifest as total abundance?

- What am I unwilling to receive that would allow more money into my life?

- What are the defining elements of my reality with money?

- If I had a lot of money, what would I be, that I am currently unwilling to be?

◆   ◆   ◆

The Willingness to Do Something Is Not the Same as Actually Doing It

During Money and Consciousness Workshops, Gary often asks people, "Are you willing to do whatever it takes to create a huge amount of money?" Most people respond, "Yes, of course!" However, when he asks them, "So, would you do prostitution for money?" then most respond with firmness and conviction, "No way." He chooses prostitution as an example, as most people have a lot of judgment attached to it. They often react to this question in an unconscious, judgmental manner. This example shows that we often misidentify the willingness to do something with the actual doing of it.

When you say you would not do something, whatever it may be, it indicates that you have a judgment that it is wrong, bad, improper, or indecent. However, when you are willing to do something, you let go of all your points of view about it and truly choose. If the decision to not do prostitution is made from choice, then it is a conscious choice. If it is made from a fixed point of view and unwillingness to receive all the judgments and everything else that might be associated with prostitution, then it is an unconscious choice. This is an example to illustrate the difference between conscious choice (I am willing to be a prostitute, but choose not to), and unconscious choice (No way, I would never do that).

Practical Process: Here are some questions that will help you to look at your decisions regarding what you are not willing to receive money for or what you would not be willing to do for money. Please give this exercise a try, even though it may seem peculiar or out of the ordinary. You may discover some interesting decisions and judgments that you have made.

- Is there anything you would not be willing to do for money?

- What kind of work or activity can you not imagine yourself doing?

- What projections, expectations, and judgments do you have that create an "I can't do it" mentality?

◆   ◆   ◆

Become Willing to Receive Everything

When we are willing to receive everything, then we release attachment to the emotions, events, or judgments that obstruct our awareness, so we have a greater clarity about what is possible.

When Steve and I did this exercise ourselves, we were amazed to discover many hidden decisions we had made about what we would and wouldn't do for money. Once we became aware of the decisions, we chose to destroy and uncreate them. Now, any time we catch ourselves thinking or saying "I would never do that for money," then we instantly destroy and uncreate that decision.

Willingness to receive does not mean that you have to physically do everything that has been asked of you or presented to you. It doesn't mean you are obligated to do something or conform to anyone's requirements. Willingness to receive everything simply means that you release attachment to the emotions, events, or judgments that obstruct your awareness, so you have a greater clarity about what is possible.

◆   ◆   ◆

Tools You Can Use to Enhance Your Ability to Receive Money—and Everything Else

Receive the greatness of you.
Questions to ask:

- What's it going to take for me to receive the greatness of me?

- What am I unwilling to receive about me that, if I were willing, would allow me to have the totality of me?

- What am I unwilling to receive about the greatness of me?

Say to yourself:

- All of the unwillingness to receive the greatness of who I truly am and all of the talents, abilities, and awareness that I decided I couldn't have, I now claim, own, and acknowledge, and I now destroy and uncreate everything that doesn't allow them to exist.

Develop the unlimited capacity to receive.
Questions to ask:

- What am I unwilling to receive here?

- What ideas or viewpoints have I created that are stopping me from receiving?

- What am I absolutely unwilling to receive that, if I were willing, would manifest as total abundance?

- What am I unwilling to receive that would allow more money into my life?

- What are the defining elements of my reality with money?

Receive everything without judgment.
Questions to ask:

- What would it be like to receive from everybody without judgment?

- What would it be like to receive everything from everybody without any point of view?

- If I had a lot of money, what would I be that I am currently unwilling to be?

- Is there anything I would not be willing to do for money?

- What kind of work or activity can I not imagine myself doing?

- What projections, expectations, and judgments do I have that create an "I can't do it" mentality?

GIFTING AND RECEIVING

In this chapter, Steve talks about the following points:

- *Gifting—the secret to experiencing the endless abundance of the universe*

- *The give-and-take program vs. gifting and receiving*

- *Letting go of the give-and-take program*

- *Tools you can use to discover the simultaneity of gifting and receiving*

Most people have been programmed to believe there has to be an exchange for everything that is given or taken. They give with the expectation of receiving something in return: "I'll give you this, and then you'll give me that." This is the give-and-take program, which the vast majority of people engage in daily. Most of us don't see anything wrong with this. It's the way we're accustomed to doing things.

Practical Process: Are you participating in the give-and-take program?

- Do you believe that if you give enough, then the other person will give back to you?

- Do you ever give people something in order to get what you want?

- Do you have a belief system that says "I give you this, so therefore you have to give me that"?

- Do you believe, "If I give, then I will get"?

   Have you ever noticed that every time you are willing to give 150 percent, then you pull someone into your life who is willing to take

---

200 percent? And they take and take until you get very upset and want them out of your life.

◆   ◆   ◆

The Give-and-Take Program vs. Gifting

The give-and-take program is vastly different from gifting. The essential feature of gifting is that no exchange occurs. When we are gifting, we don't have any expectation that the other person will give us anything in return. We gift—and in the process we receive simultaneously. When we do this, we open up to receiving from everything in the universe, not just the person we have gifted to.

I learned a valuable lesson about the give-and-take program when I attempted to assist a colleague who had been retrenched from his long-term career. I spent innumerable hours helping him to work through the many problems he had. He was constantly calling me and taking all the time I was willing to give him. He took for granted that I would be at his beck and call. In this instance, there was no real joy in my giving. I noticed that I became annoyed whenever he called, and I realized I was giving, not gifting. I saw that I had bought into the give-and-take program. Whenever we now have a conversation, I am able to be present with him without judgment. I do not feel obligated to him in any manner. This frees me to enjoy our conversations. I am now gifting and being a gift to him.

From this firsthand experience of being trapped in the give-and-take program, I learned that when I felt obligated, my willingness to give and receive stiffened up, and I created separation and barriers to receiving. When we gift, we receive simultaneously and experience the abundance of the universe. But when we engage in the give-and-take program, it creates obligation, expectation, projection, judgment, separation, and rejection.

◆   ◆   ◆

Giving to Someone Who Can't Receive

Can you imagine what it is like to attempt to give to someone who is not willing to receive? Chutisa had this point conveyed to her once when she was acknowledging an actor friend who had just won a major part in a movie. He could not receive her acknowledgment and deflected it back energetically. Since she is very close to this friend, she asked him why he was negating her acknowledgment. He apologized and told her that he had great difficulty receiving compliments without a feeling of obligation. He tended to create judgment and become suspicious of the giver. When someone complimented him, he thought, "What is the catch here? What do they want from me?" He was always on the lookout to avoid the feeling of obligation. After he talked with Chutisa about gifting and receiving, he realized that he had shut the door on many unexpected and amazing possibilities because of his unwillingness to receive.

From this experience, Chutisa realized that, like her friend, she too found it difficult to receive compliments and acknowledgment. When someone gave her praise or acknowledgment, she used to think that she had to say something complimentary in return. This give-and-take program implanted the idea that she could not receive something without being obliged to give something in return. She became aware that this was the reason she was always reluctant and unwilling to receive.

The way that Chutisa got herself out of the give-and-take program was to practice receiving compliments with gratitude. She learned to fully receive and perceive the acknowledgment instead of deflecting it. Every time anyone gave her an acknowledgement or praise, she simply said, "Thank you" with total gratitude and didn't try to return a compliment at the same time. She noticed that by doing this, she allowed people who gave her an acknowledgement the pleasure of gifting the gift without having it thrown back at them.

◆   ◆   ◆

It's Not Gifting When There Is an Obligation Attached to the Gift

I have been in situations where I was not willing to receive what was being given to me, because I perceived that there was obligation attached to it. It's not gifting and receiving when someone gives you something with the point of view of "I give you this; therefore, you should give me something in return." This is give-and-take. When you find that you are not willing to receive something due to fear of obligation, the other person is probably doing give-and-take with you. And if you are giving in order to get something in return, then you are putting yourself into a give-and-take position.

Gary suggested that to get out of the give-and-take program, we must destroy and uncreate the mindset that there has to be an exchange. We have to be willing to experience the simultaneity of gifting and receiving. We also have to let go of the idea of the exchange of energies and realize that all energy is expansive.

◆   ◆   ◆

Simultaneous Gifting and Receiving

Chutisa and I adore the idea of gifting and receiving simultaneously. We embrace it as part of our way of being and working. In our work life, we practice gifting by empowering people to become conscious creators of their own reality. We attempt to help them to make all aspects of their life fulfilling and successful. And in our personal life, we choose to do things that put smiles on the faces of the people around us without expecting anything in return. We don't do things based on obligation. We do things for people for the pleasure of doing them, without wanting anything in return. We are gifting, and, in so doing, we receive simultaneously.

In my work, I often gift information to my clients—if they request it—without expecting payment or anything else in return. The only thing I require from them is that they ask me questions. They know they can contact me anytime—as long as they ask me a question. This has, interestingly, reduced the number of calls I get that are trivial in nature. The calls I do receive are primarily for highly paid assignments. Because I am willing to be in the simultaneity of gifting and receiving, I am able to function from an unlimited point of view with my work.

One of the ways you can cultivate gifting and receiving is to practice gifting without expectation. If you start gifting without wanting anything in return, then you endorse the idea that there's abundance in the world. You will be living from the point of view that the universe is endless abundance.

◆   ◆   ◆

Tools You Can Use to Discover the Simultaneity of Gifting and Receiving

Discover whether you are participating in the give-and-take program.
Questions to ask:

- Do you believe that if you give enough, then the other person will give back to you?

- Do you ever give people something in order to get what you want?

- Do you have a belief system that says, "I give you this; therefore, you have to give me that"?

- Do you believe, "If I give, then I will get"?

- Have you ever noticed that every time you are willing to give 150 percent, then you pull someone into your life who is willing to take 200 percent? And they take and take until you get very upset, and want them out of your life.

Improve your ability to receive.
Things to do:

- Practice receiving compliments with gratitude.

- Don't try to return a compliment at the same time you receive one.

- Notice when you are not willing to receive something due to fear of obligation. Note whether the other person is doing give-and-take with you.

Let go of the give-and-take program.
Destroy and uncreate the mindset that there has to be an exchange.

Practice doing things for others without expecting anything in return.
Things to do:

- Put smiles on the faces of the people around you.

- Do things for the pleasure of doing them.

- Gift without expectation.

- Remember that the universe is endless abundance.

THE POWER OF GRATITUDE

In this chapter, Chutisa talks about the following ideas:

- *Gratitude—an essential constituent of abundance and wealth*

- *The scarcity frame of mind vs. gratitude*

- *A way get to the truth of your reactions and emotions*

- *Tools you can use to develop gratitude*

In 2004, Steve and I traveled around Australia, New Zealand, and Southeast Asia, presenting at a Leadership Boot Camp on the topic "Transforming Your Organization from a Scarcity Paradigm to Prosperity Consciousness." During these boot camps, we talked about the power of gratitude, and we asked the senior leaders we worked with to share with us their experience of gratitude in their lives. I found that most people experienced gratitude only when something they thought of as "good" happened. The more we worked with these business leaders, the more I noticed how many people misidentified what gratitude is all about.

Some of the people we worked with stated that they made a daily practice of keeping a gratitude journal. A gratitude journal is simply writing down each day the things one is grateful for. We observed that these people had a tendency to "do" gratitude as a routine act they performed without sincerity and without genuinely being grateful.

Quite a few people we know have gratitude journals packed full of shopping lists of things that they say they are grateful for. However, the lists they have compiled do not seem to translate into an energetic state of gratefulness. Please don't get us wrong. We are not belittling the gratitude journal. It is a useful tool if you are using it consciously, but it seems like a mindless act of pretense if you are not experiencing an energetic state of gratitude as you use the tool.

◆   ◆   ◆

A Scarcity Frame of Mind Keeps People from Experiencing True Gratitude

Steve and I were surprised to see this recurring misidentification and misinterpretation of what gratitude really means. We were prompted to examine the basis of this confusion and found that a scarcity frame of mind is the main perpetrator that keeps people from experiencing true gratitude. People who have a scarcity frame of mind have attitudes, mindsets, feelings, and values associated with lack or the fear of lack. They believe there is not enough to go around for everyone in the world. Scarcity becomes a way of life for them, and they often experience a feeling of lack as part of their reality. They judge that there is scarcity and lack in the world. As a result, that is what they see all around them. It is hard for them to be grateful when they assume that there's not enough and when they perceive life to be difficult.

During one of the workshops Gary conducted in Auckland, New Zealand on Money and Consciousness, a lady talked about her fear of lack, which was deeply entrenched in her relationship with money. She asked Gary, "So, what is lacking here?"

Gary replied:

> The only thing you lack is you. Everything else is total abundance. You use huge amounts of force to create a lack of you in order to create all the lacks in your life. You have a great ability to create lack. The main lack is the unwillingness to be you. Your scarcity state of mind is deeply ingrained. You have to be willing to change it before you will ever be prosperous and successful.

A scarcity mindset leads to competitive thinking. Many people believe that in order to get what they want, they have to take it away from someone else. They feel envious and resentful when someone else has something they would like to have. They believe that if someone else has something they desire, then they themselves will have to go without. They think that if they choose to do one thing, then they'll have to give up something else. This scarcity point of view encourages fear and worry. It is not easy for people to have gratitude when they are convinced that there is not enough to go around—especially when their points of view keep creating situations where they get to be right about how difficult life is! They assume that their reality of lack and scarcity is true, but nothing could be further from the actual truth.

◆   ◆   ◆

Dealing with Envy, Resentment, Bitterness, and Fear

A client of ours, Judy, worked as a solicitor in a large law firm in London. She had an intensely difficult time when she was passed over for a promotion, and one of her colleagues was made senior partner of the firm. Judy asked for our guidance to deal with the knotty feelings of envy, resentment, and bitterness, and her fear of being left behind. She described the discomfort she felt as she watched her colleague attain the kind of recognition she wanted for herself. She had a hard time being genuinely happy for her colleague. She felt confused and embarrassed by her jealousy about her colleague's success.

We asked Judy to be aware of the possibility that she might have bought into the lies and limitations of scarcity. We invited her to consider that she was not confined to her circumstance due to a deficiency of opportunities. We suggested that she might like to consider that there is enough for everyone and to see abundant prospects in everything. However, to access that true experience of abundance, she had to be willing to relinquish her erroneous belief about scarcity and lack. Instead of tormenting herself about missing out on an opportunity, we asked her to acknowledge that her apprehensions, uneasiness, and misery about the lack of opportunity were not real.

◆   ◆   ◆

Getting to the Truth of Feelings and Reactions

We recommended that Judy use an Access tool called Making It Infinite to get at the truth of her issues. We asked her to take the feelings of envy, resentment, and bitterness that she experienced and to make them infinite. We coached her to make them as big as the universe and then make them bigger than the universe. Not eternal, but infinite. When Judy did this exercise, she said that her feelings faded away and disappeared. We suspected that they would disappear since they were lies, even though Judy thought that they were true. This Access tool illustrates that when you make your feelings and reactions bigger than the universe, what is true becomes more full and substantial. Your feelings become more real.

They take up more space. And if they are lies, they dissipate. They go away. This is an awesome tool, because when you perceive that your feelings are not real, then you won't buy into them. You won't create your life based on what is not real and not true.

When Judy recognized that she had been functioning based on a lie of scarcity, then she chose to create her success rather than compete for a limited potential. When Judy did this, she ceased to be a victim of circumstances. She began to reclaim her power over her life, and she was able to see opportunities in everything. How does it get any better than this?

Since then, Judy has begun to look at what she is not willing to receive in her life. She has become aware that whatever she is unwilling to receive actually limits the amount she can have in her life.

◆   ◆   ◆

What Does Living with Gratitude Look Like?

When we work with people to help them move from the scarcity paradigm to prosperity consciousness, I am continually surprised by how many of them never consider gratitude as part of their beingness. Most people want to have more money, but do not have any gratitude for the money they already have. When people don't have gratitude for what they have and just desire to have more, then they create a sense of need. A sense of need for more money often leads to a sense of greed, which means they try to hold on to what they have as though there is never going to be any more.

Steve and I have found living with gratitude to be an essential constituent of having abundance and wealth. Living with gratitude is about having total gratitude for ourselves, for all that we have, and for our ability to generate money with ease. Living with gratitude involves living with no resistance. It is about remaining constantly open, vulnerable, and unresisting to any energy. It is about totally being and embodying gratitude. Gratitude is not just a response to attaining something we desire or expect; it is a state of beingness. It is a part of who we are in every moment.

When Steve and I first became aware that we were functioning in a scarcity paradigm, then we began to explore what it would take for us to get out of it. We discovered that to invite large sums of money into our lives, we had to first and foremost have gratitude for money and be aware of the expansiveness that money can provide. As soon as we chose to embody gratitude as a part of who we were, then we received an invitation to talk to the peak body representing the arts sector in Australia—a group with a history of functioning from scarcity. They had no budget to pay us to talk to them. However, we perceived that our presentation on prosperity consciousness could change their limiting paradigm and make a difference in the arts world. We accepted the invitation.

After that presentation, we received many calls from people who were present at our talk. They told us that they had chosen to adopt a prosperity point of view in their organizations. A CEO from Perth who had attended the session was so impressed with the ease and joy she had found in her life since she chose to live with gratitude, that she asked us to go to Perth to give a two-day seminar on prosperity consciousness for the executives and managers in her organization. This seminar was well received, and it marked the beginning of our seminars on "Transforming the Business of Your Life and the Life of Your Business through Prosperity Consciousness."

The point we are making here is that we attracted more clients and greater income because of our gratitude and our willingness to receive. We had gratitude for what we received personally in the way of more money and increased business, but we also believed in the potential of money to facilitate expansion of consciousness and change the world. Our gratitude and ability to receive enormous amounts of money, together with the ability to perceive, know, be, and receive the good that money can facilitate, have determined the circumstances and situations we have encountered in life.

These types of exquisite and extraordinary incidents regularly happen since Steve and I have made living with gratitude and receiving everything without judgment a guiding philosophy in our lives. Because we live from a place of gratitude and willingness to receive everything without judgment, we have infinite choice. Every time a "miraculous" incident occurs, we acknowledge that we have created it, with total gratitude to us and to the universe. We then invite the universe to send us more by asking this question:

• What else is possible?

◆　　◆　　◆

Gratitude Is about Receiving

Gratitude is the place in which we are grateful for everything that we are and everything that we have, with no judgment. It is impossible to be prosperous without a willingness to receive with gratitude. Gratitude is about receiving, and receiving is about gratitude. Gratitude goes hand in hand with prosperity consciousness.

When Steve and I talk about gratitude, we are talking about a state of beingness—not an action or some meaningless charade. Gratitude is a choice in every moment. Being grateful is remarkable for three reasons:

First and foremost, gratitude feels awesome. It gives us a spring in our steps and a twinkle in our eyes. Gratitude creates space and a sense of richness and aliveness so that every day becomes a celebration.

Second, when we begin to appreciate the good we have in our lives, we open ourselves up to more good. When we focus on gratefulness and appreciation, then we become aware of how all of life comes to us with ease, joy, and glory.

Third, gratitude prevents us from having a competitive mindset and a scarcity paradigm. We are able to live on the creative edge.

◆   ◆   ◆

Gratitude Booster

The bottom line is this: Whatever you focus on expands. When you focus on gratitude, what are you focusing on? You are putting your attention on what's right with your life. You are clearly focusing on what is wonderful and marvelous. Since you get more of what you focus on, you will keep getting more of what is great about your life.

When was the last time you truly appreciated the magic that you are? Make a practice of focusing on what you have, rather than on what you are missing. Stop thinking of yourself as broke. When things are not working the way you wish, instead of complaining, ask this question:

What's right about this that I'm not getting yet?

From this moment on, I invite you to look for the rightness of you and your life. Stop judging and complaining. Feel and express gratitude for you, for your life, and for everyone and everything around you all the time. You don't have to wait for something "good" to happen so you can be grateful.

I invite you to embody gratitude. Make it the state of your beingness and a part of who you are in every moment—not just a response to attaining something you desire or expect. Embodying the gratitude of you allows everything else in your life to show up. You can begin to embody gratitude by choosing to notice all that you have to be grateful for, and by expressing your gratitude earnestly without hesitation.

◆   ◆   ◆

Tools You Can Use to Develop Gratitude

Invite more of what is wonderful and marvelous into your life.
Things to do:

- Look for the rightness in your life.

- Focus on what you have.

- Express gratitude for you, for your life, and for everyone and everything around you, including the money you have.

- Appreciate the magic that you are.

- Stop thinking of yourself as broke.

- Stop judging anything.

Things to ask:

- When things are not working the way you wish, instead of complaining, ask, "What's right about this that I'm not getting yet?"

- When a "miraculous" incident occurs, be grateful to yourself and the universe. Acknowledge that you created it. Invite the universe to send more of the same by asking, What else is possible?

Use "Making It Infinite" to get to the truth of your reactions and emotions.
Something to do:

1. When you experience a feeling or reaction, make it infinite.

2. Make it as big as the universe.

3. Make it bigger than the universe.

4. Notice: Does your feeling or reaction fade away and disappear? Or does it become more full and substantial?

5. If the reaction dissipates, then it's a lie. If it becomes more full and substantial, then it's true.

LIVING IN AND AS THE QUESTION

In this chapter, Chutisa explains the following concepts:

- *The power of living in—and as—the question*

- *Asking questions creates an invitation for the universe to provide what is possible*

- *Worrying about the answer vs. focusing on the question*

- *Questions that attract the people, circumstances, and opportunities you desire*

Conscious creation is about creating by living in—and as—the question. This is an incredibly powerful attracting energy to bring you the people, circumstances, and opportunities you desire in your life.

Living in and as the question means using questions to bypass the limited answers that your mind provides. A question creates the possibilities of things, not the limitations. A question allows you to see beyond conventional concepts.

When you live in and as the question, then you engage a powerful universal force that will assist you to realize your endeavor. Questions help you to facilitate the changes you desire. They help you overcome obstacles and enable you to function from your knowing. Living in and as the question allows you to create your life with awareness.

> **If I had an hour to solve a problem, and my life depended on the solution, I would spend the first fifty-five minutes determining the proper question to ask, for once I knew the proper question, I could solve the problem in less than five minutes. Many people are looking for answers and not asking the wisest questions.—Albert Einstein**

◆   ◆   ◆

Asking Questions Creates an Invitation

Steve and I are able to create our lives more consciously when we live in and as the question. When we are faced with challenging situations, instead of becoming vested in finding answers or solutions, we cultivate an attitude of curiosity. Rather than trying to prove our answers are right, we allow new possibilities to manifest in our lives by asking questions. When we live in and as the question, then we create an invitation for the universe to provide.

Let us share with you an example of how we have used questions to create our reality. At one stage of writing this book, our accountant informed us that due to having had a very successful year, there was a large sum of income tax we had to pay within a few weeks. Previously, we would have been greatly distressed at having to pay this hefty sum of money right away in one payment. We would have become panic stricken, trying to figure out how to get more money quickly. We would have dwelled on the wrongness of the situation. We would have assumed all kinds of limited ideas such as "The only way we can get extra money immediately is by …" This would have locked us in the finite rather than allowing for the infinite possibilities that were available to us. In this instance, instead of moaning, What's wrong? we asked questions.

- How does it get any better than this?

- What's right about this that we are not getting?

These questions put us in the infinite instead of finite and allowed us to become aware of what else was possible. When we asked the question, What's right about this that we are not getting? then we started to look at what was good about the situation rather than looking at what was bad. This question asks for the awareness and unlimited capacity to perceive and receive.

Living in and as the question showed us that this tax was a recognition of how successful we had been. Instead of judging it as an imposition and a burden, we chose to celebrate it instead. By changing our perspective about the income tax, we allowed ourselves to receive more income. By living in and as the question, we created an invitation.

We then asked another question.

What would it take for at least $____ to show up with ease?

The next day, we got a phone call from an old client we had not heard from for over eighteen months. He asked us to come and shake their Board of Directors out of their self-imposed limitations. Two days later, two different organizations called, asking us to conduct conscious strategic planning workshops for them. We had never met any of these people before. Over the next week, almost daily, unexpected requests and proposals for assignments arrived via e-mail or phone. We were able to pay the taxes from what we made on just two of these jobs.

We are now willing to pay massive amounts of income tax, because that means we can receive colossal amounts of money and income. How does it get any better than this? Can you see how this works? It was clear that we immediately required more money than we had imagined. Boom! A day later, we had landed a substantial assignment that would provide extra money with ease. The next day, another two people called to engage us for workshop facilitation. What was the secret?

By choosing to live as the question, we were able to perceive outside a fixed view of reality and beyond the limited and illusive content of thought. When we asked, What would it take for at least $___ to show up with ease? then we allowed the universe to provide opportunities for that to happen. When we chose to live as the question, rather than being besieged by the problems or becoming vested in finding answers and solutions, then we allowed the universe to provide a response that was greater than anything we could determine or imagine.

◆   ◆   ◆

Don't Worry about the Answer; Focus on the Question

How many times have you told yourself you wanted to have more money and then got busy trying to figure out how to generate it? Did you end up with more money? Or did you end up apprehensive or panicky? Please recognize that "I want to have more money" and "I must have this" are not questions.

When you are not able to figure out the "how," then you may tend to assume that a situation can't possibly turn out well. Or, if you are able to create some money, but not the amount you require, then you may become disappointed, disillusioned, or upset. When you do this, you stop the money flow altogether. Instead of trying to figure things out, ask, What would it take for $___ to show up? The universe will give you opportunities for that to happen. In this way, unlimited potential and infinite possibilities will emerge in ways that you may never have imagined.

There are infinite possibilities and ways in which things can manifest. Action is just a means to an end. When you live as the question, rather than trying to figure out the answer, then you allow the universe to give you an answer. This answer is always greater than anything you could figure out. When you ask a question, things start to show up in magical ways. Questions open up new possibilities. They allow you to perceive outside a fixed and limited view of reality, beyond the limited and illusive content of thought.

Don't worry about the answer. Focus on the questions. Learn to love the questions themselves. The magic is this: If you ask questions with sincerity and earnestness, then your life itself will become a living response to them. You will start living as the question. Living as the question is powerful; if your questions are infinite and you really don't know the answers, then you set the stage for previously unthinkable leaps of consciousness. When you open up to genuine wonder, then you step out of the zone of the known and into the infinite creative possibilities of the unknown.

◆   ◆   ◆

Replacing Negative Thoughts with Unlimited Questions

By living in the question, I am able to be totally present and function in the simultaneity of past, present, and future. I am not influenced unconsciously by past events or future concerns. When I ask a nonlinear and unlimited question, and if I don't have a preconceived idea of an expected outcome or answer, then I set the stage for receiving insights otherwise unattainable.

Whenever I have negative and unproductive thoughts, feel besieged by problems, or become vested in finding answers and solutions, then I ask unlimited questions.

• What is it that I'm not getting about this?

• What am I unwilling to receive here?

• What am I pretending not to know about ___?

• What am I denying that I know about ___?

- What would it take for ___ to happen?

- What are the infinite possibilities that this will work out better than I could ever imagine?

These questions are exceptional tools for discovering the appropriate response to situations or problems. When I ask these types of questions, then things start to show up for me in different ways. The more I ask questions, the more aware I become of the options and possibilities I have.

◆   ◆   ◆

Asking Questions to Get Out of a Sticky Situation

When we were in Perth, Western Australia, conducting "Conscious Leadership" seminars, the CEO of the retail division of a major financial organization shared with us that he was disturbed by a situation related to his staff. He had just received a legal letter and was feeling depressed and bitter about the situation. We suggested that he ask himself a question.

How did I create this?

This question is helpful, because it exposes the unconscious side of a situation. However, the CEO became agitated when we suggested that he ask himself this question. He didn't like the idea that he had created the situation he was in. He thought that asking the question meant he had to take the blame for the situation.

We explained to him that the question was not about blame, shame, fault, or guilt. We encouraged him to recognize that if he was experiencing a limitation or difficulty in his life, there had to be something that he was unwilling to perceive. In truth, if anything in his life was not working, it was because he was unwilling to perceive, know, be, or receive something. Until he was able to acknowledge that he was responsible for his reality, then he didn't have the power to change it.

We suggested that he ask, How did I create this? as a way of empowering himself. We explained that he became a victim of the situation when he searched for someone to blame. He became the master of his situation when he claimed and acknowledged that he was the creator of his reality. As we worked with him, he saw that the question, How did I create this? would allow him to become open to receiving everything in his life and work, no matter what it might look like. This was a major transformation for him. He stated, "I now see more clearly what my choices are, and I feel empowered."

◆   ◆   ◆

A Question to Use on a Daily Basis

When Steve and I become frustrated with our circumstances and can't see our options clearly, we often ask this question:

How does it get any better than this?

This is a great question to use on a daily basis. Asking it is one of the fastest ways to lighten the energy of a situation. It is the ticket for getting out of the places where we are stuck.

When we find ourselves having some kind of difficulty or involved in an incongruity, or even if we are feeling agitated, weary, or out of sorts, the best way to lighten the energy is to ask, How does it get any better than this? When we use this question, we invite the universe to tell us or show us how it gets better. This is how we get out of the trauma and drama that we create for ourselves.

We also use, How does it get any better than this? when things are working out well, and we are feeling great. This question invites the universe to show us that there are infinite possibilities greater than we can imagine.

Recently, we had an amazing experience of the power of asking this question. We were planning to attend an Access workshop in Brisbane. At the last minute, we decided to leave one night earlier than planned. When we arrived and went to check into our favorite hotel, I was told that we did not have a booking until the next day. I suddenly realized that I had forgotten to change our hotel booking! The hotel manager, who knows us well because we stay at that hotel regularly, told us that he was very sorry, but he did not have a room for us. They were completely sold out for the night. I couldn't help but laugh as I asked out loud, in front of the manager, "How does it get any better than this? What else is possible?" I had no expectation of the hotel manager doing anything to fix the situation. I was asking the question so the universe could give me an awareness of what was possible.

The manager asked us to wait a moment, as he would see if there was something else he could do for us. We thought he was going to check with another hotel across town for availability. Instead, he returned with a room key and said, "Please enjoy." We expressed our gratitude to him, pleased that we did not have to change hotels. We happily took the elevator up to our room, which was located on the top floor.

When we got to the room, we discovered that the manager had given us the executive suite. We said to each other, "Wow, this is awesome! How does it get any better than this?" We immediately went down to thank the manager for his kindness. When we did, he told us with a broad smile on his face, "You are most welcome. Oh, I forgot to mention that you can have the room at the regular room rate." We thanked him again and received his gift with gratitude.

As we went up to our room in the elevator, we said to each other, "How did we get to be so lucky? How does it get any better than this?" The next morning when we went to the hotel reception to check into our original booking, there was a message from the manager saying he would love for us to stay in the executive suite for the duration of our visit. How does it get any better than this?

◆   ◆   ◆

Tools You Can Use to Attract the People, Circumstances, and Opportunities You Desire

Ask questions to create an invitation for the universe to provide.
Things to do:

- When you are faced with a challenging situation, cultivate an attitude of curiosity.

- Allow for the infinite possibilities that are available to you by asking questions.

Questions to ask:

- How does it get any better than this?

- What's right about this that I'm not getting?

- What would it take for _____ to show up with ease?

- What's it going to take to get _____?

- What's it going to take to create _____?

- What's it going to take to have _____?

- What's it going to take for _____ to happen?

Replace negative thoughts with unlimited questions.
Something to do:

- Discover appropriate responses to challenging situations and become aware of options and possibilities by asking questions.

Questions to ask:

- What am I not getting about this?

- What am I unwilling to receive here?

- What am I pretending not to know about _____?

- What am I denying I know about _____?

- What would it take for _____ to happen?

- What are the infinite possibilities this will work out better than I could ever imagine?

- How did I create this?

When things are working out well, invite the universe to provide possibilities greater than you could imagine.
A question to ask:

- How does it get any better than this?

FOLLOWING THE ENERGY

In this chapter, Chutisa discusses the following ideas:

- *Following the energy—receiving what the universe is sharing with you*

- *Letting go of control and past programming*

- *Using force and effort vs. following the energy*

- *Tools you can use to create your business, career, or work situation*

Leading yourself to money with conscious awareness is about following energy rather than using force and effort as a way of making things occur in your life.

When Steve and I began to create our business, we did it by being in control. Control meant making sure that everything happened exactly the way we wanted it to. Steve had an interesting belief that we had to work hard to create money. Much of what he believed to be true about work came from past programming that dated back to his childhood. He often insisted, "We have to be busy. We have to work hard and put in long hours." As a result, we put a lot of energy, exertion, force, and effort into our work to make sure that we were on top of everything. We made our work meaningful and significant. This is always a mistake, because whenever we make something meaningful and significant, we create commitments, limitations, burdens, and obligations. We don't allow choice in our lives. We hold ourselves captive with what we make significant.

We assumed that if we didn't put a lot of effort into promoting our business, then we couldn't be successful. We had a business plan and processes that dictated precisely what our business should look like. We spent a lot of money to print brochures and promotional materials. Since we believed that success is equal to hard work, we had an extensive list of things that had to get done every day. We put conditions, structures, and significance on our creation. With those conditions and points of view, we didn't allow anything that did not fit our fixed ideas to show up.

We were extremely busy being busy. We were using force and effort to make things happen. Can you imagine how much energy was required of us as we attempted to control everything in order to make our business successful? Enormous amounts! We were so busy controlling every aspect of our business that we limited what we could create and what we could receive. When we started to use Access tools, then we became aware that in our attempts to control everything, we were actually pitting our energy against the universe.

◆   ◆   ◆

Letting Go of Control

Once Steve and I became aware that we were doing things by control, we knew we had to observe our points of view and destroy and uncreate those points of views that were limiting us. We began to look at the unconscious conditioning that had trapped us in a cycle of hard work and dissatisfaction. We also looked at the ways we were conditioned to be in an endless chase for more.

The idea of looking at our limited points of view was not about sitting in judgment of ourselves. It was about becoming aware of how we had created our reality. What we were looking for was how to create more consciousness with our lives and how to create more money with our work. We had to train ourselves to give up being in control and instead to follow the energy.

◆   ◆   ◆

Following the Energy Is about Receiving

Following the energy is about being willing to receive the information that is available. It is about being open to what the universe is sharing with us. Following the energy involves asking questions so that the universe has an avenue for responding. The universe is an unlimited place with unlimited possibilities. It will provide unlimited opportunities and possibilities if we will ask it questions.

Steve and I have let go of doing business based on the hard work method and its step-by-step linear construct. We now create from receiving. We do this by asking the universe a question:

What are the infinite possibilities of having clients show up who are willing to pay us lots of money to help them shift their paradigms and let go of their limitations?

Since we have been asking this question, all sorts of great clients who are willing to let go of their limitations and expand themselves and their businesses have shown up.

We have also been applying the principles of following the energy and living as the question to conduct our business differently. Instead of saying, "I want my business to grow and flourish" or "I want to sell more books and audio books," we ask questions.

- What are the infinite possibilities of becoming two of the most sought-after business and leadership facilitators and keynote presenters in the world?

- What would it take for our *Conscious Leadership* book to be known to all the people who are seeking to be conscious?

- What is it going to take for our *Conscious Leadership* book to become well known all over the world?

- What are the infinite possibilities for _____ to happen?

◆   ◆   ◆

Asking Questions That Will Facilitate the Outcomes We Desire

Since Steve and I have chosen to follow the energy and live in the question instead of the answer, we have been able to function from our knowing. Learning how to ask the right question has been the most important skill we have acquired. We've discovered that we can request that the universe help us ask questions that will facilitate the outcomes we desire.

- What would it take for me to ask the right questions for this business to happen?

- What would it take for me to ask the right questions to make a great decision?

- What would it take for me to ask the right questions to get ___ accomplished?

We also choose to be open to this energy and follow it when we conduct business meetings, conference keynote presentations, and workshops. Instead of having a fixed plan or structure, we notice which direction the energy is going, and we follow it. This leads to a lot of transformation for people who attend our sessions.

Following the energy and living in the question are a much more expansive way of creating work. We have discovered that when we function from expansiveness and possibilities, those are what show up. The more we live in—and as—the question, the more opportunities are showing up in our lives.

◆   ◆   ◆

Stop Making It Significant

When I first learned to follow the energy, I became very good at perceiving the energy of everything around me. However, I used to make everything significant.

Early last year, we worked with a CEO who was having a major upheaval in his organization and in his own personal life. When Steve and I were coaching him, I could perceive his anguish, unhappiness, and distress. After every session, I was exhausted and in physical pain. After hearing Gary and Dain talk about their experience of following energy, I realized that in working with this CEO, I was making the energy that I experienced significant. I bought the pain I perceived as my own pain. When I perceived physical pain or a painful emotion, I used to create a belief that "that's the way it is," and then I made the belief solid and real.

To demonstrate my point, let us say that the people around you have the point of view that there are limited amounts of money and resources in the world. There is not enough for everyone. You perceive this point of view but rather than recognizing it as someone else's viewpoint, you buy it as real and true. You think it's a fact. You may start to believe that the problem of poverty is unsolvable. As a result, you perceive scarcity and lack in the world. Because of your perception, you create a belief that poverty and lack is the way life is. You then accept and expect that some people will have what they need and others will not.

In our work as business advisers, Steve and I have seen many organizations, large and small, conduct their business according to limiting points of view based on erroneous long-established business models. Quite often, these business practices entail traditional ways of looking at things that are not true. They are just concepts that appear to be true. For example, business people might buy into a lie like, "This is the right way (or the best way) to do things, because we've always done it this way." They then attempt to create their business based on that lie. Can they create truth out of it? Certainly not! They keep crashing into the limits of their own unawareness, which leads them to disappointment, dissatisfaction, and deprivation. Since people are usually not conscious of the reason for their limitations and disappointments, they rummage around for someone or something to blame. Frequently, they end up concluding that circumstances beyond their control are holding them back or that "it's just the way things are." Steve and I have found that when we make something significant, then it becomes solid and real. It becomes a focal point for the attraction of more of that.

◆   ◆   ◆

Practical Process: Here are some questions you can ask yourself:

- How many of the things that you have perceived about this reality in relation to abundance and money have you turned into beliefs?

- How many of these beliefs have you been unable to let go of because you decided that's the way life is?

- Will you destroy and uncreate all those beliefs, please?

- What are the infinite possibilities? (don't try to answer this question, just perceive the energy this creates for you).

Do you see what can happen when you create your life based on lies that you believe are true and significant? Fortunately, you can destroy and uncreate those lies and receive the wisdom of the universe by following the energy.

◆   ◆   ◆

Tools You Can Use to Create Your Business, Career, or Work Situation

Let go of control and receive what the universe is sharing with you.
Something to do:

- Receive the information that is available by asking the universe a question.

Questions to ask:

- What are the infinite possibilities of having _____?

- What are the infinite possibilities of becoming _____?

- What would it take for _____?

- What are the infinite possibilities for _____ to happen?

Instead of having a fixed plan, notice which direction the energy is going and follow it.

Don't make the energy you experience significant.
Things to do:

- Recognize other people's viewpoints for what they are. Don't buy into their beliefs.

- Discover what perceptions you have turned into beliefs, thinking "that's the way it is."

- Choose to destroy and uncreate those beliefs.

A question to ask:

- How many of my perceptions about this reality, in relation to abundance and money, have I turned into beliefs?

Discover questions that will facilitate the outcome you desire.
Questions to ask:

- What would it take for me to ask the right questions for _____ to happen?

- What would it take for me to ask the right questions to make the most suitable decision?

- What would it take for me to ask the right questions to get _____ accomplished?

WHATEVER YOU WOULD LIKE TO BE, YOU HAVE TO BE IT NOW, RIGHT UP FRONT

In this chapter, Chutisa talks about the following concepts:

- *Becoming what you wish to be and living the ideal of what is possible*

- *Changing your consciousness and your outer reality*

- *Creating your own reality as the key to prosperity*

- *Tools to help you claim, own, and acknowledge prosperity consciousness as a state of being*

When Steve and I began our journey toward becoming the leaders of our own lives and the creators of our own realities, then we discovered that if we wanted to be magnets for unlimited amounts of money and success, we had to become what we wished to be in this moment, right up front.

Up until this point, we had bought into the lie that we had to have a lot of money in our bank account before we could be wealthy, successful, and joyful. This point of view required us to function in a linear construct that presumed we had to *have* something (like money and time) in order to *do* something (like write a book or create more products) so we could *be* what we desired (successful, prosperous, and joyful). This is a cause-and-effect viewpoint of creation that makes use of force and effort.

We saw that we were not living the life we wished to create, because we were wasting so much of our energy and time functioning in a linear, cause-and-effect construct. We had bought the lie of this reality that said we had to *do*, in order to *have*, in order to *be*. This linear construct induced us to believe that time and money were real and that there was a limited amount of energy in this universe. We believed that, at some point in the future, when we had more money and more time, we would be free to do anything we wanted to do. Then we would be happy.

◆   ◆   ◆

Breaking Away from the Do, Do, and Do More Reality

When I was using Access processing to break away from the do, do, and do more reality, I suddenly became aware that doing, being, and having could come from a totally nonlinear point of view. I saw that I had to be willing to perceive, know, be, and receive that I was already wealthy and successful before I would ever become wealthy and successful. I know this may come across as a bizarre point of view, and yet, for me, the only thing that created freedom from the do, do, and do more reality was to perceive, know, be, and receive myself as wealthy and prosperous in the present moment. Perceiving myself as wealthy and prosperous prompted me to behave as a wealthy person.

◆   ◆   ◆

Setting the Creative Process in Motion

I set the creative process in motion by following three steps:

- First, I asked, If I had unlimited amounts of money, then who would I be that I am not willing to be now?

- Second, I became aware of what I wished to create.

- Third, I asked, What and who would I be if I had that?

Once I had the answer to the third question, I set out immediately, without further ado, to be that and to function and act from that energy.

I chose to be prosperous and successful. This was not about imagining it, visualizing it, cognitively programming it, nor fabricating some delusion that only existed in my mind. I was not creating a false universe nor pretending to be what I was not. I was not faking it nor putting on a front to create the illusion of wealth! It was not about creating a pretense of what I would look like when I was prosperous. I simply decided to live in the present and to be greater than I had been willing to be.

◆   ◆   ◆

Who Would You Be If You Had Huge Amounts of Money?

Becoming abundantly rich starts with you. You must be willing to perceive, know, be, and receive that you are abundantly rich. You must truly believe and trust that you are. Soon the conditions of your life will transform to resonate with your new level of prosperity consciousness.

Often when Steve and I say this at seminars or conferences, someone in the audience will ask, "Isn't it dishonest and untruthful when we imagine that we're abundantly rich, when we really aren't rich at the present time?"

We reply, "You're not being dishonest when you entertain the ideal of what's possible. It's not untruthful to entertain the fundamental truth of the infinite being that you are."

We have a friend who was born into a poor family. Tara never experienced luxury when she was growing up. Life didn't start out easy, and things looked pretty grim for her. Her back was against the wall, and she clearly saw that something had to change. Tara was determined to prosper and have all the luxury and opulence that rich people have. Amazingly, she wasn't focused on her poverty and lack of circumstances. She didn't tell herself, "Oh no, I'm broke. I can't afford anything."

Instead, she perceived a thriving and prosperous life, filled with success and accomplishment. She truly believed that it was possible for her to be wealthy. She trusted that she could be a millionaire.

Tara raised her level of responsiveness and receptiveness to money. She was willing to do everything possible to learn about how to handle money, how to generate it, and how to multiply it. She spent her time doing things that allowed her to see opportunities, which enabled her to increase her financial intelligence. She developed the frame of mind, lifestyle, and behavior appropriate for who and what she chose to be—and she was able to achieve her vision. She now has access to many millions of dollars and only chooses for herself those things that are exuberant.

Tara had something that other people in the same situation did not have. She had the dedication and discipline to be wealthy and prosperous. She made a demand of herself to focus her attention on being wealthy and prosperous. She didn't dwell on "poor me" or worry about "what if." She believed herself to be wealthy and prosperous. This led Tara to behave as a rich person.

Tara lives in the question and, before she chooses anything for herself, asks two questions:

- Would a millionaire choose this?

- If money weren't the issue, what would I choose?

The message here is that if you want a prosperous life, it is up to you to be responsible for achieving it. If Tara had bought the lie of scarcity as a reality, then she would have never perceived it as possible for her to become a millionaire.

◆   ◆   ◆

Making a Choice to Become Greater Than What You've Been Willing to Be

At our keynote presentations, Steve and I are often asked about the notion of making a choice to become greater than what you've been willing to be, so that you are able to create a more expanded consciousness. Another frequent question is, How can I give up the no-choice point of view and claim my power?

Tara shows us one awe-inspiring way to do both. Most people only desire to be rich and wish to have a lot of money. They think, "Wow, wouldn't it be great to be rich like those millionaires?" Or worse yet, "I could never be as rich as they are."

Tara made a *choice* to become greater than she was, and the approach she took was to ask questions.

- What are the infinite possibilities for me to be a millionaire?

- What would it take for me to be that?

- What are the infinite possibilities of this sort of money showing up in my life?

There is never a doubt in her mind as to the outcome. Tara has chosen to perceive, know, be, receive and trust that she is a millionaire. You can do this as well. You can begin this very moment. Start to realize that your worries, concerns, and beliefs about money or scarcity are not real. When you realize they are not real, then you won't buy into them and you won't create your life based on what is not real and not true.

What? You don't feel wealthy and prosperous? You don't feel like a millionaire? So, what is it going to take for you to perceive, know, be, receive, and trust that you are a millionaire? In our own practice, we have verified that if we want to be prosperous, then we must make a choice to become greater than what we've been willing to be. The truth of this is simple: When you start receiving the greatness of who you truly are, then everything in your life starts to transform. You can begin by asking these questions:

- What is it going to take for me to show up in my life?

- What is it going to take for me to receive the greatness of who I truly am?

- What is it going to take for me to perceive, know, be, and receive that I am a millionaire?

Please trust that the universe will provide infinitely if you are willing to ask, listen, and receive. You have to ask a question for the universe to give you an answer. It is no good to just say, "I want to be a millionaire."

You can duplicate the experience of Tara or other prosperous people you know by tapping into their prosperity consciousness. Tara doesn't just wish for prosperity; she has cultivated her prosperity consciousness and the attitude that she can have what she wants. You can too. Try it for yourself!

◆   ◆   ◆

Changing Your Consciousness with a Corresponding Change in Your Outer Reality

The key element of the conscious creation approach that Tara reveals in her life is that if you make a change in your consciousness, then you get a corresponding change in your outer reality. You can try this for yourself. Allow yourself to perceive, know, be, receive, and trust that you are an abundantly rich millionaire.

When Steve and I chose to be prosperous, we had to step up and make a demand of ourselves, no matter what it took, to be wealthy and prosperous. Making that demand of ourselves was essential. We made a choice to be wealthy. Once we did that, then ways of becoming prosperous started to show up in our lives.

We became aware that the ability to generate wealth is relative to our consciousness around money. It is always a choice. Do we choose anticonscious points of view that focus on scarcity, poverty, fear, resentment, jealousy, envy, and greed—or do we elevate our awareness to prosperity consciousness?

Practical Process: Envision the difference it would create in your life if you could perceive, know, be, and receive with absolute confidence that you are a millionaire. In order to do this, you have to choose to step up and become more than what you have been willing to be.

◆   ◆   ◆

Everything Is a Choice: Everything Is Infinite Possibility

Have you ever wondered what makes extraordinarily prosperous people different from ordinary people? What is exceptional about them? What makes them stand out from the rest of the crowd?

Prosperous people are not the same as resource-rich people. Prosperous people do not suffer the affliction of a scarcity mindset that shapes the lives of so many people in this world, including many rich people.

In our work with individuals of diverse backgrounds and businesses of all sizes and types, Steve and I have discovered that the primary difference between extraordinarily prosperous people and the rest of the crowd is the choices they make. Prosperous people have chosen to perceive, know, be, and receive themselves as the creators of their reality. They have claimed, owned, and acknowledged that they are responsible for their situation and the things they create. They never blame external circumstances, their past, or their background for what they are. They don't buy into the lie of scarcity and erroneous beliefs about insufficiency that are based on the appearance of poverty in this reality.

Can you imagine what kind of life Oprah Winfrey would have created if she had bought the lie of this reality—the lie that she couldn't be a famous, wealthy, and successful talk show host because she was an African American woman? Oprah said in one of her interviews that nobody could have ever imagined that she would do anything but work in a factory or a cotton field in Mississippi. From her early childhood days, people told her what she couldn't do and why. Fortunately, Oprah did not buy into their lies and erroneous beliefs. Rather, she listened to her own instinct and her knowing. She took responsibility for the way her life would turn out.

All the prosperous and successful people we know confirm that taking responsibility for being the creators of their own realities is the key to having a prosperous and successful life.

◆   ◆   ◆

Secrets of People Who Are Truly Prosperous

Many years ago, when we first returned to Australia from the United States, Steve and I had an opportunity to discuss the notion of prosperity with an amazing self-made millionaire. Edward exudes prosperity consciousness from every pore of his being. After asking him a series of questions, we ascertained what made him and other extraordinarily prosperous people different from ordinary people. They have communion with money. Edward takes pleasure in having money. He enjoys the way he acquires money, receives money, uses money, gives money, and relates to money. He is prosperous in the way he is with himself and with all things. He is truly present to the fullness and richness of each moment. He is not putting it on. It's not an image he is creating. It's the reality of who he is. Edward is a living magnet, and he invariably attracts into his life people, ideas, opportunities, and circumstances that are in harmony with his state of beingness.

Edward told us that he perceives and knows that he can create and receive an infinite amount of money every day. How does he do it? Well, that's what we are going to explore next. Hint: Edward knows that he lives in a world of infinite possibilities and abundance rather than a world of scarcity and lack. He is willing to receive everything without judgment. He is also willing to lose everything as he knows he can make more. He lives his life as though it is impossible to fail.

Edward knows and trusts something that most others don't. He perceives and knows there are infinite possibilities in this world. There is an abundance of money. There is more than enough for all, an endless supply. Edward has the awareness, trust, and knowing that all of his requirements and wishes will be fulfilled. He is not just referring to money, assets, and possessions. He is talking about everything—talents, abilities, freedom, energy, contentment, joyfulness, fun, and more. That knowing and trust allow him to live without restraint.

We are grateful for the opportunity to talk with someone like Edward, who truly has prosperity consciousness, as it prompted us to reexamine our own relationships with money. We became aware that if we would like to have something greater in our lives than striving to acquire money, then we had to begin to develop a more conscious attitude toward ourselves, toward each other, toward money, and toward communion with all things.

Steve and I have now claimed, owned, and acknowledged prosperity consciousness as a state of beingness. We know that our prosperity did not occur by divine intervention, chance, luck, coincidence, or outside influence. Aspiring to be rich, wealthy, or prosperous is not enough. Our prosperity certainly would not have happened if we had not chosen to claim, own, and acknowledge prosperity consciousness.

I ascertained that if I wanted to make some moderate and judicious changes in my life, then I could focus on altering my behavior, approach, and conduct. However, if I wanted to create a momentous quantum transformation, then I had to totally shift out of my old paradigm (the way I view myself and the world around me) and into a new one. I realized that until I began to acknowledge prosperity consciousness and to choose to become engaged in my own wealth and success, I would never be successful financially.

◆   ◆   ◆

Seeing Through the Lie of Scarcity and Lack

When Steve and I returned to Australia after two years of living with absolutely nothing, we unknowingly bought into a scarcity paradigm that afflicted other parts of our lives. For many years after our experience in the United States, we behaved around money in ways that diminished who we were, even though we both had very well paid jobs by this time. We lived in fear of scarcity and lack. We had bought into the lie that what we wanted, we couldn't get, or if we got it, we could lose it. We had inadvertently bought into the lie of scarcity, and then we tried to create our lives based on this lie.

Fortunately, we became aware that we had permitted lies about money to have immense power and authority over us and dictate the terms of our lives. We began to question the root of our distress and unease, particularly because nothing in our actual state of affairs warranted it. We discovered that the most common belief we had around money was, "We don't have enough money, and we always want more." Since we had bought the lie that there was not enough, our energy was focused on trying to rise above our perceived sense of lack, the fear of missing out, or the fear of losing to others.

At first, we were stunned to discover that we had a recurring fear about money, and we became eager to examine the cause of it. We asked ourselves a question:

What assumed points of view would we have to have, in order to have fear about money?

Our answer was, "We fear the absence of money." Our basic assumptions were "we need money" and "we need to have more money." We had bought into lies and limitations. When we saw that we had been trying to create our financial life around a lie, then new possibilities started to appear.

Instead of making ourselves crazy with worry and fear regarding the absence of money and tormenting ourselves about the need to have more, we began to recognize that our worries and distress were not real. When we were able to realize that our fears and worries were not real, then we were able to stop buying into them. We stopped creating our lives based on what was not real and not true.

◆   ◆   ◆

Becoming Aware of Our Points of View about Money and Abundance

Even though my childhood years had been full of abundance and wealth, after two years of living in the United States with almost no money, I had totally bought the lie of scarcity. It's amazing how a short period of perceived lack could grow into a full-blown scarcity paradigm and supplant any prosperity-based experiences I previously had. I had totally bought into the lies of the scarcity paradigm and was holding on to a scarcity mindset without being aware that I was holding on to it. I actually believed that the mindset was holding on to me. I became a victim of my scarcity state of mind. This is a state of beingness that vibrates with fear, lack, dissatisfaction, and frustration.

Fortunately, I became aware that my points of view about money and abundance were holding me back from realizing all that I was capable of attaining. When I saw that I was trying to create my reality around the lie of scarcity, then new possibilities started to become visible.

I rooted out my anticonscious points of view by seeing the lie of my scarcity paradigm. I discovered that the most conscious way to get unstuck from my old points of view was the opposite of what most people do. Instead of judging and beating myself up, I simply chose to see my thoughts, feelings, and emotions as an interesting point of view. I stopped trying to push these thoughts, feelings, and emotions away with energy. I gave myself a break and just acknowledged that I had those points of view. I chose to be in allowance of myself.

Most importantly, I didn't waste time and energy analyzing or looking back at my life to identify how I had acquired those limitations. To look into the past and pore over my limiting viewpoints would have only constructed a habit of looking for negative concepts that substantiated and emphasized my limitations. Analyzing and scrutinizing my past was not valuable and would only call attention to past constraints and limitations already held within me. These would simply mire me further in my own gunk and gloom. Instead, I started receiving the greatness of who I truly was, and everything in my life started to transform.

Most people want to be wealthy and prosperous, but they never truly choose to be wealthy and prosperous. There is a big difference between wanting and desiring, as opposed to choosing and making a demand of yourself. When you are unwilling to make a demand of yourself to be greater than you already are, then you get stuck in the same place you've always been and always will be.

Practical Process: Allow your awareness to go out five thousand miles in all directions to all the enormously wealthy people in the world and all the places where they are functioning and being prosperity consciousness. Tap into the place in their consciousness where they are being totally prosperous. Then bring that creative energy into your body. Notice how you feel. Begin to function from that space of beingness. See yourself already in possession of abundance, wealth, and massive amounts of money.

If you are going to perceive yourself as already being enormously wealthy and prosperous, then you have to be able to pull that energy into your body. You must fully open yourself to the energy of enormous wealth and prosperity and to the energy of what you are choosing to create. You must see yourself already in possession of abundance, wealth, and massive amounts of money. You need to have your entire being congruent with that energy. You have to consistently live and operate from that place from now on. Then, all you have to do is be willing to receive everything without judgment and allow the universe to deliver.

If you choose to have an enormously wealthy and prosperous life, then you have to consistently be congruent with the energy of enormous wealth and prosperity in every moment, from now on. It is not okay to be this occasionally or only now and then when you remember. It is not expansive for you to be this when you are eager over infinite possibilities and then to undermine your entire endeavor by sinking down time and again with doubt, negative thinking, and judgment.

◆   ◆   ◆

Tools to Help You Claim, Own, and Acknowledge Prosperity Consciousness as a State of Being

Perceive yourself as wealthy and prosperous in this moment.
Questions to ask and things to do:

- Ask, If I had unlimited amounts of money, then who would I be that I am not willing to be now?

- Become aware of what you wish to create.

- Ask, What and who would I be if I had that?

- Set out immediately to be that!

Use questions to help you perceive, know, be, receive, and trust that you are a millionaire.
Questions to ask:

- What are the infinite possibilities for me to be a millionaire?

- What would it take for me to be that?

- What are the infinite possibilities of this sort of money showing up in my life?

- What is it going to take for me to show up in my life?

- What is it going to take for me to receive the greatness of who I truly am?

- What is it going to take for me to perceive, know, be, and receive that I am a millionaire?

Make the choices a millionaire would make.
Questions to ask before you choose anything:

- Would a millionaire choose this?

- If money weren't the issue, what would I choose?

Try these practical processes.

Things to do:

- Envision the difference it would create in your life if you could perceive, know, be, and receive with absolute confidence that you are a millionaire. In order to do this, you have to choose to step up and become more than what you have been willing to be.

- Allow your awareness to go out five thousand miles in all directions to all the enormously wealthy people in the world and all the places where they are functioning and are being prosperity consciousness. Tap into the place in their consciousness where they are being totally prosperous. Then bring that creative energy into your body. Notice how you feel. Begin to function from that space of beingness. See yourself already in possession of abundance, wealth, and massive amounts of money.

BEING OUT OF CONTROL, OUT OF DEFINITION, AND OUT OF LIMITATION

In this chapter, Steve discusses the following ideas:

- *Taking yourself out of autopilot*

- *Living a life scripted for you by someone else vs. creating your life*

- *Giving up the no-choice reality*

- *Tools you can use to begin consciously creating your life*

How do you want to live your life? Are you aware that if you don't claim and own your power, then you create a limited possibility? Many people create their lives by living out other people's reality. They do this by working in occupations chosen by their families or by making choices because of societal influence or "excellent prospects." I would like to tell you about Chutisa's early conditioning. She experienced firsthand what it feels like to live a life scripted and prescribed by others.

Chutisa was told as a very young child that she must become a scientist. She was persuaded to go to a university to attain degrees in microbiology and bio-chemistry. She was told that this was the only way she would become a successful and valuable person, and she bought this point of view. After three years of study-ing microbiology and biochemistry, both of which she absolutely loathed, Chut-isa found that nothing in her life seemed to be going right. Perhaps it is more accurate to say that nothing was really wrong, but she was feeling miserable and disgruntled. Her whole life experience began to gnaw at her.

Chutisa became aware that if she wished to have a joyful life, then she would have to choose differently. She chose to stand up for herself, and she took a mam-moth step toward becoming the creator of her own reality, even though she was deemed to be letting her family down. She took herself out of autopilot and asked questions.

- What is going on here?

- What is it going to take for me to get out of this situation?

She became willing to be out of the control system of her current reality and to stop living by other people's rules and regulations. She stopped worrying so much about what others thought and became more aware of her true talents, abilities, and potential. She recognized that she had within her the power to do whatever was necessary to change the things that were not serving her.

She became willing to be out of control, out of definition, out of limitation, and out of form, structure, and significance with her former reality. In other words, she claimed and owned her own power and began to consciously create her own life. If Chutisa hadn't claimed the totality of her capacity, she would still be creating her life from a limited point of view and experiencing only limited possibilities.

I'm not sharing Chutisa's history with you so you'll think that she is cool (although she really is!). I'm using her story to illustrate that we all have an infinite capacity to experience the greatness of who we are. We don't have to buy into the limited points of view and perspectives that are all around us. It is possible to create our lives the way we would like them to be. Yet most people will not allow this into their awareness.

So, would you please claim and own the capacity to celebrate your life and make it a joyful experience every day, starting today? And would you please claim and own the ability to be out of control and to relate to life in spontaneous interaction with the energy of the moment?

◆   ◆   ◆

Do You Create Your Life from Obligation?

While we were writing this book, I got a call from Jonathon, a forty-something general manager of a successful business based in Adelaide, South Australia. Jonathon was having a problem with obligation and longed to break out of the limitations he had imposed on himself. He felt a strong sense of obligation to his uncle, who had given him his job at a time when he desperately needed the money to pay his large credit card debt. Jonathon became a general manager of the business and felt duty bound to remain in the job, which he disliked, because he didn't want to disappoint his uncle. Jonathon saw his work as obligation. His job was something he felt he had to do, not something he chose to do.

When Jonathon came to see us, he was miserable, despondent, and discouraged. I asked him these questions:

- Is this the life you would like to have?

- Have you made a choice in life—and lived as if there were no other choices? Do you create your life as if you have no choice in it?

As he considered these questions, I sensed that Jonathon was struggling with the personal accountability and responsibility they entailed. After what seemed to be an eternity of silence, Jonathon said, "Oh dear! You are absolutely right. For the most part, I have been creating my life as if I had no choice in it." Jonathan's life had become drudgery, because he was not doing the things he loved. He loved to paint, but his job working in his uncle's business was extremely well paid, and he didn't feel he could quit. I asked Jonathon to reflect on the questions:

- What would it be like to give up your current reality and your no-choice attitude?

- Are you willing to give that up?

Although Jonathon declared that he would like to stop creating his life as if he had no choice, he found it challenging to take full responsibility and accountability for being the creator of what was actually showing up in his life. In order for him to let go of his limitations, he had to recognize that everything in his reality was a creation of his choice. I asked him some more questions to encourage his awareness:

- What are you creating?

- What choices are you making to limit your expansion?

- Do you feel responsible for your own creation?

By asking himself these questions, Jonathon became aware that he had shut down a large amount of his perceiving, knowing, being, and receiving in order to live his no-choice reality.

◆   ◆   ◆

Are You Staying in a Job You Hate?

Are you one of those people who stay in a job you hate because you think that you have no other choices? Do you keep doing your job only because it is paying you a massive sum of money? This was forty-two-year-old Mandy's modus operandi for two decades. However, her willingness to give up her no-choice point of view has changed all that. Mandy started to recognize that she could choose differently when she asked herself these questions:

- Will money, no matter how gargantuan an amount, ever compensate me adequately for staying in an uninspiring job that is depriving me of my joyful expression of life?

- Am I selling myself short?

Mandy loved to write stories and enjoyed creating incredible science fiction novels, but her commitment to her grueling work as a highly paid corporate accountant allowed her no time to write. Mandy had allowed money to be the beginning and end of her work life, with satisfaction falling by the wayside. She eventually began to feel tyrannized by her job. Things began to change for Mandy when she decided to consciously create her life.

I am not suggesting that you negate and judge your current job. Nor am I suggesting that you should all of a sudden get up and walk away from the work that you are doing. However, I am encouraging you to find out what you truly love to do. Discover your unique talents and abilities and become aware of the unlimited opportunities to implement them and generate huge amounts of money as well.

Practical Process: Ask yourself these questions:

- What would happen if you were out of control, out of definition, and out of form, structure, and significance in creating your fabulous, unbelievable, wealthy life?

- Would you live to experience the joy of your life?

- Would your life be about celebration—not diminishment?

◆   ◆   ◆

Tools You Can Use to Begin Consciously Creating Your Life

Take yourself out of autopilot and begin asking questions.
Questions to ask:

- What is going on here?

- What is it going to take for me to get out of this situation?

Break out of your self-imposed limitations and obligations.
Questions to ask:

- Is this the life I would like to have?

- Have I made a choice in life—and lived as if there were no other choices but that from then on?

- Do I create my life as if I have no choice in it?

- What would it be like to give up my current reality and my no-choice attitude?

- Am I willing to give that up?

Recognize that everything in your reality is a creation of your choice.
Questions to ask:

- What am I creating?

- What choices am I making to limit my expansion?

- Am I being responsible for my own creation?

- Will money, no matter how gargantuan an amount, ever compensate me adequately for staying in an uninspiring job that is depriving me of my joyful expression of life?

- Am I selling myself short?

Recognize you can choose differently.
Questions to ask:

- What would happen if I were out of definition, and out of form, structure, and significance in creating my fabulous, unbelievable, wealthy life?

- Can I live to experience the joy of my life?

- Can my life be about celebration—not diminishment?

DO WHAT YOU ENJOY IN LIFE

In this chapter, Steve talks about the following concepts:

- *Discovering what you love to do—claiming your innate talents*

- *Working to make money vs. doing what you love*

- *Living in ten-second increments*

- *Tools for discovering what you love to do*

When you do what you love, the money will follow with ease.

This message really struck home for Chutisa and me during a meeting with Gary while we were writing this book. This is the insight that came through loud and clear in our conversation with Gary.

To create abundant money, we must first acknowledge, claim, and own our innate talents and abilities and see how we can best use them. We have to be willing to claim, own, and be everything we are, as the outrageous, wonderful beings we are. When we start receiving the greatness of who we truly are, then everything in our lives starts to transform, including our financial resources.

◆　　　◆　　　◆

Discovering What We Love to Do

When Chutisa and I chose to create our business, we made it our priority to discover what we enjoyed in life and what we loved to do. It had to be something that would nourish and fulfill us and at the same time allow us to generate huge amounts of money.

Virtually all successful artists, celebrities, and athletes who have embodied their greatness have the absolute confidence and trust that come what may, they will one day reach the pinnacle of their professions. These people are able to perceive, know, be, and receive what they really enjoy in life. They know what they love to do. They are aware of who they are, what they are in love with, and what they wish to accomplish. This is what gives them their extraordinary positions in the world.

When Chutisa and I do what we love, then money flows more rapidly toward us, as long as we are not operating in the scarcity paradigm. When we are doing what we love, we aren't working just for the money.

We are inspired by the example of Steve Jobs, the CEO of Apple Computer, who discovered what he loved to do early in life. He and his friend, Steve Wozniak, started Apple in Jobs' parents' garage when Jobs was twenty. Within ten years, Apple released what Jobs calls "our finest creation," the Macintosh, which grew into a $2 billion company with over four thousand employees. Then, just after Jobs turned thirty, he was fired from the company he founded.

What happened? As Apple grew, Jobs hired a CEO. Jobs and the new CEO did well together for the first year, but their visions of the future began to diverge. They had a falling out, and the Board of Directors sided with the CEO. At age thirty, Jobs was ejected from the company he had founded. He was devastated and didn't know what to do. What had been the focus of his entire adult life was gone. It was a very public failure, and he thought about running away from Silicon Valley.

But he realized that he still loved what he did. He decided to start over. As Jobs tells it, he didn't see it at the time, but being fired from Apple was the best thing that could have happened. "The heaviness of being successful was replaced by the lightness of being a beginner again, less sure about everything. It freed me to enter one of the most creative periods of my life."

During the next two years, Jobs started two companies, NeXT and Pixar. Pixar created *Toy Story*, the first computer-animated film and became the most successful animation studio in the world. And then, in an unexpected move, Apple bought NeXT, and Jobs returned to Apple. The technology developed at NeXT became the heart of Apple's current renaissance.

Jobs said, "I'm convinced that the only thing that kept me going was that I loved what I did. You've got to find what you love. And that is as true for your work as it is for your lovers."

Your work fills a large part of your life. Like Jobs, we believe that the only way to be truly satisfied in life is to do what you believe is great work. As he said, "The only way to do great work is to love what you do." Jobs tells people who haven't yet found what they love to keep looking. His advice is, "Don't settle. Keep looking until you find it. As with all matters of the heart, you'll know when you find it."

To create abundant money in this reality, start with you.
You have to first do what you enjoy in life.
You have to do what you love to do.

◆　　◆　　◆

So, What Do You Love to Do?

Every year Chutisa and I consult with individuals and businesses around the world, helping them to attain greater freedom, greater consciousness, and greater awareness of their potential, abilities, and capabilities. In doing this, we've discovered a very interesting pandemic: A lot of people have no clue about what it is that they love to do!

If there is one question that we are asked constantly, it's this one: "How can I discover my right path in life?" When people ask us this question, we can accurately predict that they are not truly satisfied with their current circumstances.

I often ask them these questions:

• Do you love and truly enjoy what you spend most of your time doing?

• Is your life a celebration?

• Is your life enjoyable and pleasurable, or dreary, monotonous, and lackluster?

• Do you feel there are infinite possibilities and unlimited opportunities to generate wealth, or do most opportunities for you seem to have gone?

Most people respond that they really are not happy in the work they are doing. They are doing their current jobs just for money.

It is not how much we do but how much love we put into the doing. It is not how much we give but how much love we put into gifting.—Mother Teresa

◆　　◆　　◆

Do What You Love and the Money Will Follow

Oprah Winfrey has demonstrated that when you choose to do the things that you love, the money will follow. Oprah, who is one of the richest people in the

United States today, has enlivened the lives of millions of people worldwide through her television program. She pursues the work she loves. Oprah is successful because, from the beginning, she has not been defined by dollars or motivated by money. She declared that she would do what she is doing even if she weren't being paid. She said that she was just as excited when she was earning only $100 per week and doing what she loved as she is now. She became unstoppable. Furthermore, money has flowed rapidly and with ease toward her. The contributions made by Oprah and her television show are endless, because money is power. Oprah uses her power to do a great deal of good in the world.

Most people who embody prosperity consciousness similar to Oprah Winfrey's have become exceptionally wealthy, because they have chosen to do what they love. They have provided goods and services that benefit the world at large and have been justly rewarded in return.

◆　　　◆　　　◆

All Things Are Possible

Have you ever known anyone who generated a fortune doing what they disliked, who truly enjoyed the experience? Have you ever seen exceptionally successful athletes, actors, or artists who hate what they do? There you have it—one of the secrets to becoming successful, rich, and famous. To be successful, you have to do what you enjoy in life. All things are possible. You are an unlimited being. You have unlimited possibilities.

Gary Douglas, the founder of Access Energy for Transformation, exemplifies a way of being that affirms the truth that all things are possible when you choose to do what you love with conscious awareness. For Gary, the foundation of a successful business is consciousness. What's more, he truly enjoys his work, travelling around the world helping people to become more conscious and more aware of what they wish to create in their lives.

Gary also enjoys working with animals, especially horses. He loves showing people how to be in communion with their horses and to perceive the horses' energy and interact with them at that level. His experience has led him to pioneer an approach that facilitates the expansion of consciousness for both horse and rider. His work with horses has now been created as a TV series.

Gary didn't approach his idea for creating a TV pilot using the normal step-by-step linear construct. Instead, he expressed a dedication to creating a TV show, he asked questions, and he was not vested in the outcome.

- What are the infinite possibilities for this to happen?

- What would it be like to do that?

- What would it take for that to happen?

A friend who is a producer and director told Gary what it would take to create a TV pilot. Gary's response to that information was not "I've got to raise money before I can create the pilot." Instead he asked more questions.

- Hey, universe, can I have this?

- What would it take for the money to show up?

Gary talked about the idea of the TV pilot in his workshops. Within two weeks of conceiving the idea, the people and money he needed began showing up. Within six weeks, he had the necessary money and the people to produce the pilot. The pilot, called *Conscious Horse, Conscious Rider*, was completed within eight weeks from the time he conceived the idea.

So, what is the point of this story? The point is that things become possible when you choose to do what you love with conscious awareness. Gary was able to create a TV pilot that took only eight weeks from conception to completion. He didn't do this by deciding how it was supposed to be. He did it by living in the question, following the energy, not being vested in a certain outcome, and receiving what was given.

Even though Gary works with business people around the world, he is never focused on money, nor vested in the outcome of his work. He enjoys himself enormously, simply because he knows that if he does what he loves, then the money will follow. Making a profit is not his primary purpose, yet he attracts more money than some who work purely for money and profit. Gary advises people to never take a job they don't like, nor put up with conditions that make them unhappy. He reminds people that the moment they accept a job out of desperation for survival, all they are going to ever get is survival.

◆   ◆   ◆

Is Your Life Enough for You?

Chutisa and I have met a lot of people who are struggling to make ends meet and using force and effort as a way of making things occur in their lives. Many people we know stay in uncreative, stifling jobs to make money, out of the belief that this is necessary for survival. We've worked with many clients who have stayed at undesirable jobs for years, and sometimes forever, because they felt they had no choice.

The tug-of-war between the desire to do rewarding work and the need to make more money is played out daily across the world, even in the lives of many rich and famous people. Recently, while facilitating a conscious leadership seminar for a group of high-profile CEOs and senior executives from major organizations in Sydney, Australia, I asked these questions:

- What does your job mean to you?

- What do you desire of your job that if you didn't desire would let you be free?

From the front of the room, a perfectly groomed senior executive from a major corporation stood up to share his response to my questions. He said he believed he had to take his job because of his financial needs. He assumed that he had to accept the job that had been offered to him because he might not get another one. He worked consistently to obtain money, because he thought he had to do this to survive.

I asked him two more questions:

- Is there limitation in that point of view?

- Is your life enough for you?

It came through loud and clear to him that he was rigidly maintaining the point of view that he had no choice but to work at the place he did, so that he could eat at opulent restaurants, wear expensive clothes, drive a luxury car, and pay the soaring mortgage payments on his great house. This senior executive stayed in a job he hated, because he believed there were only a limited number of jobs that would pay him the money he required. He could see no other way to have everything he needed to survive.

There were three assumptions in this particular point of view. The first assumption was that he must survive. The second assumption was that he could not survive without money. The third assumption was that he was unwilling to not survive. He was fixated on survival. And that is exactly what he created for himself: survival from paycheck to paycheck, even though his paychecks were enormous.

◆   ◆   ◆

If Money Were Not an Object, Would You Do the Job You Are Doing Now?

I asked this senior executive an important question:

If money were not an object, would you do the job you are doing now?

He seemed very surprised when he heard himself reply, "Certainly not!" Nevertheless, he lamented that he felt stuck. He said that he didn't know what else he could do to make money. He said, "I have no idea what it is that I would truly love to do. How can I find out?"

My advice to him was to live in the question and ask questions like these:

- What would it take for me to discover what it is I love to do?

- What does the universe require of me?

- What does the world require of me?

- What do I require of me?

  I also suggested that he ponder these questions:

- What is the one thing that I can do so easily that it takes no effort?

- If money were not the issue, what would I choose?

This executive called us a month later with great excitement. He wanted to let us know about his insights into what he would truly love to do. He said that he was excellent at taking photographs that captured the essence of his subjects, and he had already exhibited a lot of his photographs. This was so much fun and so easy for him that he treated it as a hobby. He now realized that he could actually make a lot of money out of his love of photography. He had thought nothing of his natural talent and his love of photography until we had asked him to ponder the question, What is the one thing that I can do so easily that it takes no effort?

Practical Process: If you don't know what it is that you would love to do, then ask yourself the following questions before you choose to be, do, and have anything. They will help you to make choices based on what is best for you.

- What is the one thing that I can do so easily that it takes no effort?

- If money were not the issue, what would I choose?

Practical Process: Imagine that you are told that you have only one year to live and that you will be in perfect health up to the last day. However, one year from today, you will leave this world.

- Would you continue to do what you are currently doing?

- Would you continue to live where you are?

- Would your daily routine change?

- Would you spend your time differently?

- Would you hang out with the people you are with currently?

- Would you do things differently?

- Would you treat yourself and others differently?

- Would your priorities change?

- Is what you are doing today so exuberant for you, that you can imagine doing it until the day you die?

◆   ◆   ◆

Two Questions to Ask Every Morning

Chutisa and I approach our work every morning with these questions:

- If today were the last day of our lives, would we choose to do what we are about to do today?

- Would an infinite being choose this?

Whenever the answer has been no, we consciously look at what else is possible.

◆   ◆   ◆

Living in Ten-Second Increments

Living in ten-second increments is an Access tool for living in the present moment. It is an awesome tool that helps us to live in the present moment and create our lives with consciousness. By living in ten-second increments, we become the conscious navigators of our own realities. Ten-seconds is a chunk of time short enough and also long enough to highlight that we make choices constantly. Everything we do is a choice, and living in ten-second increments reminds us that we can choose differently in every ten seconds. Everything is a choice. We constantly ask ourselves this question:

If I had ten seconds to live the rest of my life, what would I choose?

When I introduce this notion in workshop presentations, someone in the audience will invariably ask, "How can you do business in ten-second increments? Isn't this being frivolous and reckless? Would this not create chaos in your life?" From frequently hearing this question, I realized that most people misidentify and misapply the meaning of living in ten-second increments as being flippant and lacking focus.

Living in ten-second increments is not about being without control or lacking focus. Quite the opposite, it's about focusing totally on what is happening in the moment. I become much more in command of our business when I am fully focused and engaged in what I am doing. I noticed that when I do everything in ten-second increments, I seldom make a wrong decision. This is because my mind doesn't wander, and I don't operate on autopilot.

As an adviser to leaders and businesses, I have found that when I focus my attention in ten-second increments at a time, I become aware and conscious during those ten seconds. I give my clients my complete attention. I have the capacity to understand their requirements, and I am able to provide all that is required.

When I live in ten-second increments, I am able to know what is important for me, and I act on that knowing. I am not functioning from obligation, projection, expectation, and judgment. Before I chose to live in ten-second increments, I used to create my life and business based on obligation. I used to think that once I had made a decision or commitment, then I was obligated to fulfill that decision even when it no longer worked for me. I thought I had to. I thought I was obligated, and if I didn't do it, then people might be upset or disappointed with me. I bought the idea that everybody else was more important than I was.

Since Chutisa and I have put into practice the art of choosing our life in ten-second increments, we have found that we create more choice and greater opportunities to receive money. We have stopped functioning based on obligation or apprehension about missing out on opportunity. Living in ten-second increments is a great tool for us. It helps us to choose from the work assignments that have been offered to us. We have stopped accepting work based on a sense of obligation, the fear of missing out on future opportunities, or the amount of money that we will receive.

We ask each other this question every day:

If we had ten seconds to live, would we want to do what we are about to do today?

Whenever the answer is no, we know we need to choose differently. The question, If we only had ten seconds to live, what would we choose? is one of the most important tools we've encountered to help us make the big choices in life. When we use it, all external expectations, projections, judgments, significance, apprehension, and trepidation about embarrassment or failure fall away.

Practical Process: Over the next twenty-four hours, choose to live in ten-second increments. Before you do anything, ask yourself the following questions:

- If I had ten seconds to live, what would I choose?

- Make it a point to pay attention to these things:
  - Where does your time go?
  - How do you spend your energy?
  - Where do you focus your thinking?
  - Where do you focus your feelings?
  - Where do you focus your action?
  - How do you respond to the opportunities that come to you?

- At the end of the day, see for yourself how much more focused you have become—at work, at home, everywhere.

◆   ◆   ◆

Tools for Discovering What You Love to Do

Ask yourself whether you are truly satisfied with your current circumstances.
Questions to ask:

- Do I love and truly enjoy what I spend most of my time doing?

- Is my life a celebration?

- Is my life enjoyable and pleasurable or is it dreary, monotonous, and lackluster?

- Are there infinite possibilities and unlimited opportunities to generate wealth, or do most opportunities seem to have gone?

Give up the viewpoint that you have no choice but to work at your current job.
Questions to ask:

- What does my job mean to me?

- What do I desire of my job that if I didn't desire would let me be free?

- Do I believe I have to keep my job in order to survive?

- Is my life good enough for me?

Discover what you truly love to do.
Questions to ask:

- If money were not an object, would I do the job I am doing now?

- What would it take for me know what it is I love to do?

- What does the universe require of me?

- What does the world require of me?

- What do I require of myself?

- What is the one thing I can do so easily it takes no effort?

- If money were not the issue, what would I choose?

Remember that you have choice!
Questions to ask:

- If today were the last day of my life, would I choose to do what I am about to do today?

- Would an infinite being choose this?

Use questions as tools to discover what is possible.
Questions to ask:

- What are the infinite possibilities for _____ to happen?

- What would it take for _____ to show up?

Live in ten-second increments.
Questions to ask:

- If I had ten seconds to live, what would I choose?

- If I had ten seconds to live, would I want to do what am I about to do today?

LIVING ON THE CREATIVE EDGE

In this chapter, Chutisa explores the following ideas:

- *Living on the creative edge—the art of conscious creation*

- *Creating is about asking and receiving*

- *Trying to make things happen vs. living on the creative edge*

- *Tools you can use to consciously create your life*

Have you ever found yourself working unpleasantly hard and putting a lot of force, effort, and energy into trying to make things happen? You may not even have been aware you were doing it. Most people misidentify and misapply what it takes to make things happen. They assume that they've got to do hard work!

- Can you imagine what it would be like if you didn't have to do hard work?

- Are you willing to allow a constant flow of money and prosperity into your life?

Making things happen doesn't take hard work. All it takes is choice, trust, and the ability to live on the creative edge. The ability to live on the creative edge is the vehicle that will allow you to lead yourself to money with consciousness.

◆　　◆　　◆

What Does Living on the Creative Edge Mean?

So, what does living on the creative edge actually mean? It means having the ability to receive everything. People who live on the creative edge recognize their oneness with the universe. They know that the universe will provide infinitely if they ask and are willing to receive. Mother Teresa, who did amazing work with the poor in India, totally exemplified what it is like to live on the creative edge. She created entirely by asking and receiving. She was the living embodiment of compassion and made the most of her unique talents and abilities for the greatest benefit. She had three cents when she began to create her organization, The Missionaries of Charity. In her desire to serve the world's poor, she claimed, owned, and acknowledged no limitations, not even church policy. She had a strong sense of purpose that moved her and kept her inspired in the face of hardship.

Mother Teresa did what she loved. She consciously chose her work and life's path by receiving everything without judgment. She also lived in the question. She asked herself and the universe a truly important question that propelled her on her path: "How can I know whether this is the right path for me?"

The answer she received was, "You will know by your happiness." This answer guided her choice at the beginning of her career and for the rest of her life. Her love of her work allowed her to build the Missionaries of Charity into a worldwide, billion-dollar organization.

She was able to accomplish her charitable work through generosity of spirit and the simultaneity of gifting and receiving. She became one of the most powerful women in the world because of her compassion and her willingness to receive everything and to lose everything. Isn't this a paradox?

Although Mother Teresa had taken vows of poverty, chastity, and obedience, she was definitely not operating from a scarcity paradigm. She was able to build a billion-dollar organization dedicated to helping the poor. Mother Teresa walked with presidents, prime ministers, kings, and queens in order to accomplish her work. She was featured on the cover of almost every important newsmagazine in the world. She received many honors and became known as one of the most powerful women in the world. She was able to accomplish great work, because she was willing to receive what the universe was sharing with her. She was willing to live on the creative edge.

◆　　　◆　　　◆

Starting to Live on the Creative Edge

In our experience, choosing to live on the creative edge is essential for creating abundance. Most of our clients are successful leaders who have clarity about what they want in life. Many of them even have an understanding about what has been blocking them. However, most of them don't have the awareness or the tools to create with ease the things they truly wish to create. They often use a lot of effort and even resort to struggling, in order to create what they want. Many of them admit that, even when they struggle, they are not able to create what they desire.

Steve and I empathize with our clients, because we ourselves have been there and done that. We fully understand the reason why these people are not yet living the life that they would like to create. We know firsthand what it feels like to waste energy and time functioning from a linear construct.

Many years ago, before Steve and I were introduced to the idea of living on the creative edge, we used to think that we had to use a lot of energy and actively do things to get what we wanted. This was a cause-and-effect viewpoint of creation that required force and effort. We had bought into the lies and limitations of linear constructs as we were growing up. We tried to create plans and systems for the future based on making the "correct" choices or decisions, which we thought would put everything right in our lives forever. When we bought into these false points of view, then we created limitations that didn't allow us to live on the creative edge.

One way of starting to live on the creative edge is to begin to create your life as a present-time adventure instead of a future possibility. I'm going to share with you a very subtle but powerful Access tool for living on the creative edge that may well change the rest of your life. It has certainly changed ours.

To begin to live on the creative edge, we invite you to let go of the idea of the step-by-step linear construct of your reality. Do you currently create your life with beliefs that resemble the following two statements? "I've got to have a good job that pays a lot of money." Or "That will give me the freedom to do any thing I want to do, and then I will be happy"? If so, then create your life instead by living in—and as—the question. If you want anything in your life to be better or to be different, then all you have to do is ask the universe to assist you. Then, you must be willing to receive what the universe is sharing with you and you must remain open to the infinite possibilities.

◆   ◆   ◆

Living on the Creative Edge Is about Receiving

The essential point here is that living on the creative edge is about receiving. It is also about awareness and the ability to access infinite possibilities and universal knowledge beyond your own imagination and experience.

Albert Einstein is another good example of someone who lived on the creative edge. His work and achievements did not come from his cognitive ability, but from living in and as the question.

The important thing is not to stop questioning.—Albert Einstein

By living in and as the question, Einstein was able to access universal knowledge. He questioned the whole notion of time, proposing that speed would allow us to travel beyond the present. He refused to be constrained by the finite potential of this reality. Einstein once said, "The most beautiful experience we can have is the mysterious. It is the fundamental emotion which stands at the cradle of true art and true science."

◆   ◆   ◆

Creating Your Reality

Let me share with you how Steve and I created our realities by living on the creative edge. Six years ago, Steve gradually came to the recognition that he had been creating his life and work based on the erroneous point of view that, to be successful, he had to have all of the trappings of a reality that included a high salary, a lofty reputation, status, and ownership (shares) in a business that created wealth. Once he realized that he had been trying to create financial wealth based on a linear construct of this reality, then he recognized that this was expansive neither for him nor for our relationship. He realized that this was not what he truly desired. When Steve saw that he'd been trying to create his financial life and work around the lie of the scarcity paradigm, then new possibilities started to appear.

During this time, I was working as a usability specialist and transpersonal change counselor, helping individuals and businesses to become more conscious and more able to deal with everyday pressures in demanding environments. One morning while we were walking along the beach, Steve asked me these questions, which instantaneously changed our work and life path.

• What would it be like for us to work together in our own business?

• What is it going to take for that to happen?

We both knew immediately that it would be awesome and expansive for us to work together, and we set out to create it.

When we first set up our business, we had many points of view about how we could create it to be exactly the way we wished it to be. We had many great ideas, and we decided over a few months exactly what our business was going to look like. And then, we set out to create our business in the generally accepted and long-established tradition of business, using control and force to make sure we were on top of everything. We used huge amounts of energy and effort to control everything and ensure our business and our lives happened the way we had decided they should. We put conditions on our creations. With those conditions, we did not allow anything that did not match them to show up. Fortunately, we became aware that by controlling everything, we were limiting what we could create and what we could receive. We began to ask this question:

What else is possible?

Get a Sense of What You Wish Your Life, Work, and Business to Be

One day during a conversation, Gary shared with us the way he created Access as a business. He explained how he created by receiving, rather than by using control, force, and effort. This was an inspiration to us. We saw what it would take for us to create our business consciously.

When Gary was establishing his business, he began by getting a sense of what he wished his life, work, and business to be. He didn't just think it; he got the feeling of it. He got the vision of what his life, work, and business would look like and what they would feel like. He felt the vibration of all the elements he wished to have in his life and work.

He then stuck a little bubble out in front of him containing those elements. He pulled energy into the bubble from all over the universe until he felt it growing stronger. Then he let little trickles of energy go out to all those people who might be looking for him and didn't know it.

Every time he encountered an opportunity that had the feelings or energy of his vision, he went for it, whether it made any sense to him or not. When an opportunity didn't have those feelings, he didn't go there. If a situation or possibility had some of the elements that he desired, but not all of them, then he didn't go there, either. Gary did a lot of different things, and each thing he did led him closer to developing Access as it is now. His business has been hugely successful. Access has grown exponentially over the last fifteen years and continues to expand and flourish.

♦   ♦   ♦

Destroying and Uncreating Our Business

The idea of creating from receiving really resonated with us, so, from that moment on, Steve and I made a choice to create our business and our lives from receiving instead of through control. Once we made the choice to create from receiving, we began straight away to recreate our business. The first thing we did was to totally destroy and uncreate our business as it was.

When Steve and I present the Access process called Destroy and Uncreate at seminars and workshops, some of the participants invariably state, "This is far-fetched, implausible rubbish and hogwash!" I am not going to try to convince you otherwise. It's your choice to believe it or not. I had difficulty believing it myself at first. All I can tell you is that, even though the notion seems weird, wacky, and bizarre, it works like magic. Let me share with you our experience of Destroy and Uncreate.

Destroying and uncreating our business did not mean we actually had to physically destroy anything. It did not mean we had to close up or actually end the business. It did not mean that we had to tear down our business, wipe out our lives, or eliminate our relationship. What we destroyed and uncreated was everything we had made significant about the past—everything we had made real and solid. We destroyed and uncreated our decisions, conclusions, and judgments about the way our business was supposed to be, the way we should operate it, and our ideas about the expected outcomes.

This process is critical, because as soon as people decide that they are at the peak of their business and "this is as good as it gets," then they will not be able to create anything that surpasses that judgment. Whenever we decide that we have something right in our lives, then we stop receiving.

We also destroyed and uncreated our obligations, projections, expectations, disappointments, struggles and regrets, as well as our need to compete and our decisions about what was going to happen in the future. When we destroyed and uncreated everything we had created in the past, what showed up was the opportunity to create something totally new. This practice put us on the creative edge of things. So, how did we destroy and uncreate our business? We simply made this declaration to ourselves:

Everything our business and our lives were yesterday, we now destroy and uncreate them totally.

This made space for us to start creating our business and our lives anew, without the baggage of what had been.

For instance, when we were first setting up our business, Steve refused to present leadership training and development workshops. He didn't see the benefit of the traditional leadership training process. For years before we set up our business, he had been a CEO and a board director for many organizations and had participated in a lot of leadership training programs himself. He didn't like the way typical leadership programs trained leaders to manage and control staff with force, effort, form, structure, and significance. He resisted and reacted to anything to do with leadership training.

At the same time that we were destroying and uncreating our business as it was, Steve chose to destroy and uncreate his points of view about leadership. This freed him up to co-create with me the conscious leadership philosophy that has become a major part of our work. This process enabled us to stop defining and categorizing what we would be and do as business consultants.

We remained open to the infinite possibilities. We became willing to receive anything that came our way, including leadership training assignments. Since we destroyed our unwillingness to present leadership training, we have perceived other possibilities for training leaders to lead with conscious awareness. Our business has doubled in size over two years, and now over one third of our business is related to conscious leadership and consciousness in business.

◆   ◆   ◆

Conscious Creation

Having destroyed and uncreated our business as it was, we then recreated our business anew. We began by choosing what we would like our lives and our business to be. We used the following questions to get a vision and perceive the energy of the business we wished to have:

- What would a business that facilitates expansion of consciousness and allows us to make gargantuan amounts of money look like or feel like?

- What does the universe require of us?

- What does the world require of us?

- What do we require of us?

- What do we want out of life?

- What would we choose to do if money was no object?

- What would it be like to do it?

The vision is more than just the picture of what it's going to look like. It is the feeling of what it would be like to have this business and what it would be like to do this work. This is not the same as visualization. In my experience, visualization is limiting, because it is a function of the mind and the imagination. My imagination can only define what I already know, but by shifting the focus away from the picture and toward the vibration, I transfer energy from my perception of the picture, which is limitation, to the infinite possibility.

Rather than trying to figure out how to create our business, Steve and I became aware of what we would truly like to achieve in our lives. We did this by asking this question:

What would it be like to consciously create our life?

This envisioning process isn't about the "how;" it is about what we would like to have and what it would feel like to have it. It was vital to stop limiting ourselves with a focus on, How is this or that going to happen? The "how" creates the need to figure it out, and the need to figure it out creates a constraint.

We got the awareness that we would like a business that allowed us to generate huge amounts of money, currency, and prosperity consciousness. We wanted to travel magnificently around the world, helping organizations, leaders, and individuals reach a higher level of consciousness and become more aware of what they would like to create in their lives. Above all, we wished to create a business that was able to assist and empower people to move out of a scarcity paradigm and into prosperity consciousness. The awareness I have just described is the energetic vibration of these elements—not a mental image.

Instead of seeing the picture, we tuned into the vibration of the components that would bring what we desired to fruition. Once we ascertained the basic vibration, then we put it out there in front of us. We then pulled the energy into it from all over the universe until we could feel it growing stronger. We then let a little energy trickle out to all the potential clients who were looking to have what we could facilitate. From then on, we just followed the energy. We didn't try to control it. We were willing to let it show up. Now, every time we come upon projects that match the vibration of these elements, we choose to do them. When we encounter clients who match this vibration, we choose to work with them.

When something shows up that feels like this energy we move in that direction. When something doesn't have that feeling, we do not choose to go there.

◆　　　◆　　　◆

What Are the Infinite Possibilities?

Once we started recreating our business and our lives using this process of conscious creation, things got a lot easier. What's more, everything has been coming to us more with ease, joy, and glory. Once we became aware of what we wanted to achieve and what it would be like and feel like to do that, then we became much more aware and alert to the various prospects and opportunities that showed up. All we have to do is be willing to receive the information that is available.

Sometimes conscious creation is spontaneous. Recently, we were in an airplane coming home from Sydney, where we had been assisting the leadership team of a large not-for-profit organization move from a scarcity paradigm to a more prosperity-conscious way of governing their organization. I said to Steve, "It's really inspiring to see people experience transformation and change. What are the infinite possibilities for more of this to happen?" Steve replied, "That would be awesome. What would it take for that to happen?"

When we went to our office the next morning, there was a message from one of our treasured clients in Brisbane, asking us to come to Brisbane in three days to work with their board of directors on the topics of prosperity and scarcity and governance, almost exactly the same as the previous client. Furthermore, during the afternoon of that same day, we received an urgent call from a conference organizer in Sydney, pleading for us to make a keynote presentation the following week. Our experiences illustrate what we mean by conscious creation and creating by living in and as the question. When we truly ask for something and know that we will get it, it always shows up for us. It's not about controlling what, when, where, and how it shows up, or having an expectation that it will show up instantaneously. It's about allowing it to show up and being willing to receive it when it does.

◆   ◆   ◆

Creating Ourselves Anew Every Day

Another important aspect of conscious creation is starting every day anew. We start the day by asking two questions every morning:

• Who am I today?

• What grand and glorious adventures am I going to have this day?

  When we go to bed, we say:

• Everything I believed I was and everything I created today, I destroy and uncreate it all.

• Who I was today, I destroy and uncreate.

  Often this is not said out loud, but we perceive the energy of these statements and tap into it. This process is about unlocking where we have been programmed to operate instead of creating based on infinite possibility. It opens things up for us to create our reality from a different place.

  By asking the question, Who am I today? we consciously destroy and uncreate everything we were yesterday. When we destroy and uncreate our fixed points of view about what we thought we could be, do, have, create, and generate, then we allow ourselves to show up as far greater than anything we ever thought was possible.

  We also destroy and uncreate our business, our relationship, and our financial situation every day by saying:

• Everything our business was yesterday, we now destroy and uncreate.

• Everything our relationship was yesterday, we now destroy and uncreate.

  By practicing this, we are able to create ourselves, our lives, our relationship, and our business anew in the moment. When we ask, What grand and glorious adventures are we going to have this day? then we allow ourselves to perceive, know, be, and receive the infinite possibilities for ourselves and for everyone concerned.

◆   ◆   ◆

Seeing Possibilities

In order to live on the creative edge, we had to be willing to perceive, know, be, and receive what would be enjoyable and gratifying about having our business the way we envisioned it. For instance, I feel exuberant and uplifted whenever I reflect on how people will be able to move from scarcity into prosperity consciousness when Steve and I work with them. I feel energized and enthusiastic whenever I reflect on what our existing clients have told us about the expansion of awareness and prosperity they've experienced from working with us.

Conscious creation continues to be the single most useful process I have ever encountered on the topic of creativity. This way of living on the creative edge has been my ever-ready friend in every possible kind of situation. Steve and I constantly apply this tool and philosophy in all aspects of our business. It has helped us to develop new products, services, and workshop programs. We ask the universe to give us an insight and inspiration into what it would take for us to develop seminars, services, and products that would give us multimillion dollars in revenue.

To heighten our abilities to perceive infinite possibilities, we ask ourselves:

What must we also perceive, know, be, and receive that would allow us to recognize unlimited potential and expand our business with ease?

Many of our best opportunities were created out of situations that other people perceived as ordinary, everyday events. Our business grows and continues to flourish, because we have developed the capacity to see possibilities where others saw difficulties or complications.

Living in the question has enabled us to access and trust our intuitions and to create new services for our clients. At the same time that we have been writing this book, we have also been creating podcast productions on consciousness in business. This new service will assist leaders and organizations to be more extraordinary, especially when they are under pressure. How does it get any better than this? The simple philosophy of conscious creation is "ask and receive." It's very light! I am amazed at how effortless it is to live on the creative edge. We create our lives every moment as though everything is a miracle! How does it get any better than this?

There are two ways to live your life.
One is as though nothing is a miracle.
The other is as though everything is a miracle.—Albert Einstein

What comes up for you when you read the message above? Can you imagine what it would be like if you could create your life moment by moment? Creating a magnificent and magical life starts with you.

◆   ◆   ◆

Tools You Can Use to Consciously Create Your Life

Rather than using force, control, and effort, create by receiving.
Things to do:

1. Get a sense of what you wish your life, work, or business to be.

2. Get the vision of it.

3. What would it feel like?

4. What would it look like?

5. Feel the vibration of all the elements you wish to have in your life or your business.

6. Put a bubble out in front of yourself containing those elements.

7. Pull energy into the bubble from all over the universe.

8. When you feel it growing stronger, let little trickles of energy go out to all those people who might be looking for you who don't know it.

9. Every time you encounter an opportunity that has the feelings or energy of your vision, go for it.

10. When an opportunity doesn't have those elements, don't go there.

11. If a possibility has some of the elements you desire, but not all of them, don't go there.

Destroy and uncreate your business and your life.
Say to yourself:

• Everything my business and my life were yesterday, I now destroy and uncreate them totally.

• Everything I believed I was and everything I created today, I destroy and uncreate it all.

• Who I was today, I destroy and uncreate.

Recreate your business anew by choosing what you would like it to be.
Questions to ask:

- What would a business that facilitates expansion of consciousness and that allows me to make huge amounts of money look like, or feel like?

- What does the universe require of me?

- What does the world require of me?

- What do I require of me?

- What do I want out of life?

- What would I choose to do if money was no object?

- What would it be like to do it?

Create yourself anew every day.
Questions to ask:

- Who am I today?

- What grand and glorious adventure am I going to have this day?

PROSPERITY CONSCIOUSNESS
IS A CHOICE

In this chapter, Chutisa discusses the following ideas:

- *Choosing prosperity consciousness—exercising the power of choice*

- *Becoming aware of the story of your personal spending*

- *Showing up as the infinite being you are*

- *Tools to help you choose prosperity consciousness*

Many years ago, Steve and I began to explore what it would take for us to get out of the scarcity paradigm and into prosperity consciousness. We discovered that, contrary to what a lot of people think, prosperity is not about having massive amounts of wealth and possessions. It's not just about money, resources, and assets we can collect along the way. Prosperity consciousness is not directly related to the amount of money people have. Rather, it is the communion they have with money, material wealth, themselves, others, and all things. It's about the way they treat themselves and others and about the abundance they are willing to perceive, know, be, and receive in the world.

Steve and I know many people who have gargantuan amounts of money and material wealth, yet they are totally embroiled in a scarcity state of mind. They have been tainted by the scarcity paradigm and its greed, self-indulgence, and mistrust. They have damaged their relationships with others because of money. We have come across many business owners who are anticonscious around money. They have vast resources but use money as an instrument of control, to have power over people.

We are privileged to have participated in the world of successful businesses and to have been associated with extremely wealthy people. We have had many opportunities to witness the ways people do not seem to relate well to money, even when they have a lot of it. After observing our clients' ways of relating to money, we began to question the root of their distress and unease around money, particularly because it seemed so unwarranted. From discussions we've had with clients and colleagues, we have learned that even among those who are extremely wealthy, one of the most common beliefs around money is, "I don't have enough of it. I want more."

◆   ◆   ◆

A Chronic Sense of Insufficiency

People who don't have prosperity consciousness have a chronic sense of insufficiency about life. This is the fundamental mode from which they think, act, and function in the world. Steve and I have very wealthy friends who don't have prosperity consciousness, even though they are making seven-figure incomes. These people have large amounts of money with no debt, and they are still plagued with the fear that someday their wealth will disappear. They are so ensnared in the scarcity mindset that they make choices in life that don't bring them happiness.

Many of our wealthy friends choose to stay in careers that have them joylessly working twenty-four hours a day, seven days a week. They spend their days doing jobs they don't really want to do, just to make more money. Even when they have lots of money, they still aren't happy or relaxed about it. They always mull over the negative what-ifs: What if I lose my money on this transaction? What if I fail? What if I can't come up with the money for ___? What if I am unable to come up to scratch? They are besieged by a hundred fears and judgments that make them despondent.

When we go out to dinner at expensive restaurants with these friends, they make comments about how expensive the meals are. We find that their comments tend to detract from our enjoyment of the moment and our appreciation of the meal. Quite often, we find ourselves buying into their scarcity mindset and focusing on the cost of the meal as well. We noticed that when we focus on what a meal costs, then we start judging and justifying its worth, and the whole experience becomes stressful. If we buy into other people's bogus points of view about scarcity, then we create limitations that do not allow us to expand into what is possible with money.

♦   ♦   ♦

Interesting Point of View: Being in Allowance

Now whenever we find ourselves in this type of anticonscious situation around money, the moment we feel the negative energy welling up inside of us—and before the energy totally seizes us up—we defuse these points of view by saying to ourselves:

- That's an interesting point of view.

- Interesting point of view I have this point of view about money. (This phrase allows us to observe our own points of view without judgment. It brings us to an awareness of the point of view we have).

These statements release the energetic attachment we have to the point of view and free us from it.

Every time we hear someone's viewpoint about money, we choose to instantly acknowledge that it is only an interesting point of view. It does not have to be our reality. It does not have to be what occurs. When someone comes at us with a strong point of view, and we choose to say to ourselves, "Ah, interesting point of view," then we shift the consciousness of the world. This occurs because we have not bought the point of view. We have not made it more solid, we have not gone into agreement with it, we have not resisted it, and we have not reacted to it. We have not made it a reality. We have allowed reality to shift and change. We call this Being in Allowance.

♦   ♦   ♦

Making It Infinite

Sometimes, however, we don't catch ourselves at the early stage of buying in to someone's point of view about money. The negativity has already run through us and taken hold of us energetically. When this occurs, instead of reacting automatically to our emotions, we choose to make them infinite. How do we do that? We take whatever point of view we have about the situation and make it infinite. We do this by first feeling the energy of the point of view and then expanding it to a size greater than the universe. At this point, the point of view just disappears.

This is done by awareness. There is no specific action that has to be done. The point of view vanishes as soon as we choose to make it infinite.

When we make our money worries and our scarcity points of view infinite, they fade away and disappear. This occurs because when we make a false point of view infinite, we are opening our consciousness to it, and it drops away all by itself. It is as though we are removing the lid from a pressure cooker. Magnify the point of view to infiniteness, and it becomes like empty space. If your worry about money is a lie, it will disappear.

It works the other way for what is true. When we make something that is true infinite, it becomes more full and substantial. It feels more solid and valid. It takes up more space. If it is the truth, it becomes more substantial.

◆   ◆   ◆

What Happens When People Do Not Change Their Consciousness about Money?

Time and again, we have found that people who don't have prosperity consciousness tend to play out beliefs from their upbringing about worthiness, value, and money. Unfortunately, they cling to their old thoughts: That's just the way life is. There's no way out. There are no other choices.

One client said to me, "I always have enough to survive. I don't really need any more than this to make it. I may not be rich, but I'm happy." I've heard this excuse from people in every part of the world. They have a tendency to get ensnared in unconscious and limited thinking. This prevents them from seeing opportunities all around them.

There has been much discussion based on the precepts of prosperity consciousness that if all the wealth on the planet were divided up and redistributed equally among everyone on Earth tomorrow, and no one changed their consciousness about money, all the money and resources would be back in the hands of the original owners within a few years. The originally wealthy people would be wealthy again, and the poor people would be poor again.

A follow-up study of million-dollar lottery sweepstakes winners in Canada illustrates this point. The study found that the vast majority of sweepstakes winners were broke within five years of receiving their prizes. Their money consciousness had not developed to the point where they could benefit from their winnings for very long.

Most of these winners believed that as soon as they won the lottery, they would be free of their poverty way of being. They believed that when they won the lottery, they would do everything they had always wanted to do. The truth is, they did not need to wait for their conditions to change in order to be conscious of abundance. Right now is the time. Because those lottery winners didn't change their essential relationships with money, they had the same degree of limitation and financial mess after they won the lottery as they had before. The only difference was that the mess was larger.

◆   ◆   ◆

Become Aware of the Thought Patterns That Sabotage You

A powerful way to begin to change your life and become prosperous is to start noticing what you expect to experience in life. Be aware of the consciousness you have about money. If you are honest with yourself, then you will intuitively and instinctively perceive and know whether or not your relationship with money is expansive and conscious.

Have you ever wondered what it would take to know exactly what you are doing and thinking that is getting in the way of your having more wealth? When Steve and I work with clients, we help them to become aware of the thought patterns and points of view that sabotage them without their even knowing it. We repeatedly observe the same pattern in people who do not have prosperity consciousness: thoughts of scarcity and insufficiency lead to actions of constraint and result in a lack of essential outcomes.

Practical Process: The first step to changing your relationship with money is awareness. Below I have listed several common ways that people sabotage their wealth potentials. If you're sincere about having more money in your life, then please reflect on how you spend a typical day in conjunction with money. What are you doing and thinking in relation to money? Most people are usually doing one of the following: working hard for it, spending it, worrying about not having enough of it, planning what to do with it, or avoiding any discussion or thoughts about it. See if you do any of these things:

- Do you often give money supremacy and control over you by attaching emotions to money?

- Do you worry about money when you look at your bank account?

- Do you function from the idea of spending money instead of creating money?

- How do you feel when you spend money?

- Do you throw away your money by spending it as a way to try to be happy or as a way to try to survive?

- Do you feel guilty every time you spend money? Do you spend out of fear, which produces lack, or do you spend with empowerment, which produces more?

- Do you care more about spending money than having it? If you think money is about spending it, then what is the likelihood that you will have it?

- Do you often feel apprehensive and reticent about asking for money that is due to you?

- Are you diffident and hesitant when you must receive, ask for, or speak of money?

- Do you make choices based on cost only, rather than quality?

- Do you allow money to do all your choosing for you?

- Do you worry about paying for an event that may be happening in the future?

- Are you concerned about paying bills you expect to receive?

- Do you consistently think stressful thoughts about money?

Practical Process: Here are some other things you can pay attention to as you become more aware of your mindset about money. Do you gift freely of yourself? Is it hard for you to receive? Your attitudes toward money are often indicative of your attitudes toward life itself.

- Pay attention the next time you pull out your wallet or checkbook. Are you spending from a sense of loss or are you gifting?

- Listen to what you are saying to yourself as you hand out money.

- What is your attitude about gifting?

- When is it easiest to gift?

- When is it hardest to gift?

- Listen to the inner voice ringing in your ears during your money transactions.

What is it going to take for you to become aware of the story lines of your personal expenditures? If you can look closely at how you use your money and how you feel when you spend your money, then you will be able to discover exactly how you relate to it. Do you have many interesting excuses and justifications? Do you often say, "I need to spend money because _____ (fill in the blank)"? The story of your personal spending can tell you a lot about the paradigm you are functioning in. The way you function with money dictates how you handle difficulties, respond to situations, and conduct all aspects of your life.

◆   ◆   ◆

Letting Go of the Scarcity Mindset

We have a colleague, a prominent forty-something wealth creation expert, who applied his knowledge of property development to generate wealth beyond his imagination. Even though his bank account was growing rapidly, his consciousness was still stuck in the scarcity paradigm. This kept him from perceiving and experiencing his huge wealth. He often felt a chronic concern, or even fear, that he would never really have enough, generate enough, or be able to keep enough money.

Our colleague called us after attending the launch of our book, *Conscious Leadership,* in Melbourne last year. He said that he got an insight into his limitations as a result of our conversation at the book launch. He wanted us to help him to destroy and uncreate his limitations. We agreed to advise him. When we began working with him, he realized that even though he was proficient at creating a lot of money, he was not able to enjoy his wealth because of the scarcity mindset he was functioning in. He believed these fallacies: More is better. There is not enough for everyone, so I'd better hurry up and take mine now before someone else does.

This kind of "neediness mentality" led him to be acquisitive, self-indulgent, and stingy. His scarcity state of mind kept him from perceiving and experiencing the ongoing natural state of abundance. Our colleague clearly demonstrated that money and success alone could not promise a gratifying and contented life.

He was entirely focused on accumulation and acquisition. His mindset was that it is better to have more. He was focused on what he didn't have, instead of what he could create. He spent much of his time thinking about what he didn't have enough of and trying to figure out how he could acquire more. This created a sense of need, and it always led to greed. Greed meant that he tried to hold on to what he had, as if what he had was as good as it was going to get. This neediness mode became the lens through which he saw the world. We asked him a question:

Does this mode of thinking make you feel lighter? What's the truth here?

He responded, "No, it feels very heavy." We explained to him that if something made him feel heavy, then it was a lie for him, whether or not it was true for anybody else. The truth, we said, would always make him feel lighter. A lie would always make him feel heavier.

◆   ◆   ◆

Truth and Lies

We recommended that our wealth creation expert use an Access tool called Truth and Lies to spot the lies of scarcity that he was functioning under. The principle behind this tool is that whenever our attention is stuck on something, there has to be a truth—as well as a lie—attached to it. We suggested that he could sort out the lies from the truth by asking this question:

What part of this is true, and what part is a lie, spoken or unspoken?

We also advised him that the majority of lies that stick our attention are unspoken lies.

Our wealth creation colleague was unaware that he had been functioning in a scarcity paradigm all his life. He was not able to step out of that paradigm by simply generating a lot of money, since he was modeling someone else's rules of wealth creation. He had been programmed to believe that it is better to have more, and he kept thinking about his financial affairs in terms of "I don't have enough" or "I need more." We told him that if a thought kept coming back, then he should ask himself this question:

What part is true?

We explained that realizing the answer to that question would make him feel lighter. Following that, he should ask himself this:

What are the lies, spoken or unspoken, that are attached to it?

Our client thought about this. He was able to see what was limiting him from having true prosperity when he discovered these unspoken lies: There is not enough money for everyone. There is never enough.

He became aware that his energy had been focused on trying to rise above this perceived sense of lack and the implanted fear of missing out and losing to others. When he spotted these lies, the whole thing turned loose. The Truth and Lies process helped him to see the lies of scarcity that had been hanging him up. He was able to recognize that neediness was the emotion from which he had been creating.

Our wealth creation colleague recognized that if he wanted to enjoy his wealth, then he had to stop functioning based on the lies of the scarcity paradigm. We advised him that he could use Truth and Lies on an ongoing basis to become aware of all the other unspoken lies of the scarcity mindset, which had been his primary mode of operation.

◆   ◆   ◆

Perceive, Know, Be, and Receive

After doing the Truth and Lies process, our wealth creation colleague told us that he wished to continue to develop and expand his prosperity consciousness. He recognized that no matter what actions he took to generate enormous wealth—and even if he possessed huge sums of money—he would never be truly prosperous unless his consciousness changed. Everything would remain the same. He would still have persistent anxiety about not having enough.

We invited him to use the Access tool known as Perceive, Know, Be, and Receive, to unlock his limitations around money. We suggested that he ask the following question thirty times a day for at least three days:

What must I perceive, know, be, and receive that would allow me total clarity and ease with money, prosperity, and abundance?

This question started to unlock the places where he had created his life as the limitation it had become. It enabled him to start making his life a celebration. He now looks for the joy of life instead of the despondency and insufficiency. He is creating a whole different reality. How does it get any better than this?

Steve and I use this tool on a regular basis to change any area of our lives that is not working the way we would like it to work. This simple process constantly helps us unlock our limitations. We like to use the long version:

Perceive, know, be, and receive what I refuse, dare not, must never, and must also perceive, know, be, and receive that would allow me total clarity and ease with ___.

We put anything we're concerned about in the blank: issues relating to money, job, relationship, investment, or staff.

◆   ◆   ◆

To Choose or Not to Choose—Your Choice

Steve and I have met many people who manage to attract large sums of money but are not able to retain the energy or make their money expand. They are stuck in the scarcity paradigm and are always focused on being broke or poor—or trying to not be broke or poor. It doesn't matter how much money they have in their lives. If they are holding on to a scarcity state of mind, then they will never be anything but poor—because that is what they have convinced themselves they are.

No one sets out in life to be permanently broke. No one could possibly intentionally desire a lifestyle of poverty and failure. So, why do people assume a lifestyle of scarcity, which for some reason becomes permanent? We are living in an abundant universe. Why can't these people seem to get out of their poverty trap? Even when they receive unexpected handouts, they find ways to get rid of them quickly. Money never seems to stay with them for long. They are always waiting for their external circumstances to change or finding reasons why they can't possibly prosper.

Steve and I had this message harshly demonstrated to us once when we were attempting to assist a friend who was having financial difficulties. We loaned him a substantial sum of money to clear his credit card debt. We also offered him other tools and recommendations that we knew would be helpful to help him look at how he created his money problems. He turned down our offer. When we asked if he had been working with the tools and recommendations we had provided, he said, "Well, no, not really." He didn't have time. He was too busy. It was too hard. He didn't think the tools were suitable for him. He couldn't imagine how they would work in his situation. What he really needed was more money so he could get out of the financial predicament he was in again. He had many justifications for why his life was the way it was.

At first I did not allow myself to truly perceive the truth of where our friend was sitting. I got sucker punched by him time and time again, because I was unwilling to look at what he was doing that was not expansive and not good. I made the mistake of thinking that because he asked us to help him clear his credit card debt, he also wanted to get clear of his scarcity mindset and become conscious.

It didn't take us long to realize that no matter how much money we were willing to give our friend, he would spend it immediately. He would be back, asking for more, with no intention of paying it back. He had expressed no interest in getting out of the poverty lifestyle, even though his financial situation had gone from bad to worse. He refused to emerge from the box that he had trapped himself in. We recognized that his choice was to be anticonscious with money and with the way he created his life. He didn't choose to be aware of the things he did. It was his choice. We acknowledged his choice without judging it as right, wrong, good, or bad. We did not try to impose our point of view on him. Instead, we asked him some questions that encouraged him to be aware of his choices.

- What do you want out of life?

- What would it take to have everything in your life expanding exponentially?

- What would you do with the money?

- How do you use money?

- What are you unwilling to receive about money that, if you were willing to receive, would allow you to create great amounts of money in your life?

We are grateful for the valuable experience we had with our friend, because it prompted us to examine some important questions.

- Why can't some people get out of the poverty trap?

- What strips them of the power to change?

- What are the differentiating factors between truly prosperous people and those with a scarcity mentality?

We embarked on a journey to discover what the fundamental differences are between people who have plenty of wealth and people who always have a short or ephemeral supply of riches. Through our inquiry, exploration, and investigation, we discovered once again that it has to do with *choice*.

◆　　　◆　　　◆

Exercising the Power of Choice

We discovered that, unlike prosperous people, people who function in the scarcity paradigm do not exercise their power of choice as a way of life. In fact, most people who have a scarcity mindset are not aware that they have choices at all. They don't know that they can choose the quality of their lives. The scope of what they can attain is limited by their lack of awareness and by what they fail to choose. Because they are not aware of what they don't know, there is little they can do to change. To them, change is unimaginable! These people cannot and will not acknowledge that they are the creators of their realities. They have crafted their lifestyles according to their own financial sob stories. These are the stories that give their lives meaning and significance. They have created their lives by their stories, and they are on a mission to prove to the rest of the world that their lives suck.

Our friend with the money problems was addicted to his own trauma, drama, and unconsciousness around money. He had a propensity to dwell in the scarcity mindset. He has focused on lack and blamed his financial condition on poor market conditions, health, natural disasters, or other external situations. He was not willing to do what it takes to change his life. Sadly, our friend had built his financial sob story on a pile of lies. He was no longer aware of the lies he was telling about his finances to keep his stories going. The more he stuck to his financial sob story, the more his story became solid and real. His reality was not one of abundance. It was one of scarcity and lack. And it was his choice!

Our friend was drawn toward the comfortable habit of worrying and tormenting himself about things outside his control. He was focused on what he couldn't do. He was waiting for conditions beyond his control to improve. He made decisions based on what he thought he wanted, but he was not open to what was possible. He had created his reality from "I want more money."

◆   ◆   ◆

"I Don't Want Money"

In our experience in working with clients and with ourselves, Steve and I have learned that when we think or say, "I want ___," we are actually saying, "I lack." We may think we "want" something, but most of the time, this sentiment is an indication of the scarcity paradigm at work. When we say we want something, we are judging that we don't have enough of it. This is often an indication of how we feel that we, ourselves, are not enough. When we think that we are not enough, then we try to make up for that internal sense of lack and insufficiency by wanting things we see around us. The word "want" is a key element of the scarcity paradigm.

Gary recommended that instead of creating from "I want money," that we create from "I don't want money." He explained that every time we say, "I want money," we're actually saying, "I lack money"—and that's exactly what shows up in our lives. Whatever it is that you focus on, that is what you will get more of. When you focus on "I lack money," you will feel yourself going into an unconstructive and uncreative mode. From this place, there is no solution. When you focus on the "lack," you'll get more of that lack.

If you don't like what you are getting, then you will have to change your thinking. Gary suggested an experiment to help shift your paradigm. Say this statement ten times:

I don't want money.

If you're like most people, then saying "I don't want money" will make you feel lighter, because when you say it, you are saying "I don't lack money." This is where things start opening up for you. When you start saying "I don't want money" and acknowledging the truth that you don't lack money, then you will draw money to you.

◆   ◆   ◆

Out of Scarcity and into Prosperity

Steve and I discovered that to become prosperous, all we had to do was choose prosperity consciousness. Prosperity consciousness is a choice, just as the scarcity paradigm and anticonsciousness are choices. Prosperity consciousness is easily accessible to all who would like it, if they perceive and know that they can have it and are willing to receive and be it.

You might be thinking, "That's easier said than done. How do I choose prosperity consciousness when I feel stuck in the scarcity paradigm?" Or maybe you know what you need to do, but can't seem to do it. If you don't like being stuck in the scarcity paradigm, why would you keep focusing on it and choosing it?

To choose prosperity consciousness, you have to pay no heed to what you find objectionable about your financial situation. Instead, you have to focus on the unlimited alternative possibilities and what you would like to create. When Steve and I started to do this, we began to perceive and receive many new opportunities. We were able to act on them regardless of what our reality concerning our financial situation had been up to that point. So, what is it going to take for you to make a choice to be greater than your present situation? What's it going to take for you to expand your prosperity consciousness?

Practical Process: Get a sense of what it would be like to be conscious and to have prosperity consciousness. Ask yourself this question: What would I be, if I were being the infinite being I truly am?

◆   ◆   ◆

Showing Up as the Infinite Being You Are

If you are going to be conscious and prosperous, who do you have to be? The answer is you have to be yourself. You have to claim and own the capacity to show up as you—the infinite being you actually are! When I first heard that I had to claim and own the capacity to show up as me, the infinite being, I was uncertain what this actually meant. I used to have the idea that to be an infinite being, I had to be faultless, flawless, and superbly perfect in every way. I thought it meant that I had to behave in a certain way. I was making the idea of being an infinite being very significant.

It takes a lot of energy to make something significant, and, in doing so, I became bewildered. But instead of giving up, I kept asking myself three questions:

- What would I be, if I were being the infinite being I truly am?

- What is it going to take for me to claim and own the capacity to show up as me, the infinite being?

- What are the infinite possibilities for this to happen with ease?

I had no clue how it was going to happen or what it would look like. I just kept asking those three questions.

These questions helped me to realize that claiming and owning the capacity to show up as me is the same energy I experienced as a little kid, when I was willing to just be me. When I was a kid, I was not out to impress anybody. I didn't try to do anything. I was just being the infinite being I truly am. I was willing to have communion with everything around me. I was not putting up barriers to receiving anything. This is what the energy of "showing up as me" feels like. It's not about pretending or becoming something I am not. When I was able to perceive what the energy felt like, I was able to embody it. I began to become prosperous at the moment I chose, for myself, to *be*. Prosperity consciousness is about right here, right now. It occurs in the moment I choose to be all that is possible.

Abundance, prosperity, and wealth are always available to you, but you have to choose to make yourself available to them. Are you willing to receive and to claim, own, and acknowledge that you are worthy of abundance, prosperity, and wealth?

◆   ◆   ◆

Tools to Help You Choose Prosperity Consciousness

Be in allowance.
Say to yourself:

- That's an interesting point of view.

- Interesting point of view I have this point of view about money.

Use "Making It Infinite" when you encounter negative points of view.
Things to do:

- Take your negative point of view about a situation and make it infinite.

- Feel the energy of the point of view and expand it to a size greater than the universe.

- Because it is false, the point of view will vanish as soon as you decide to make it infinite.

Become aware of the thought patterns that sabotage you.
Things to do:

- Notice what you expect to experience in life.

- Be aware of your consciousness about money.

Use "Truth and Lies" to spot the lies of scarcity.
Questions to ask:

- Does this belief make me feel lighter?

- What's the truth here?

- What part of this is true, and what part is a lie, spoken or unspoken?

Discover the truth of thoughts that keep coming back.
Questions to ask:

- What part of this is true?

- What are the lies, spoken or unspoken, that are attached to this thought?

Use "Perceive, Know, Be, and Receive" to unlock your limitations around money.
A question to ask and something to say to yourself:

- What must I perceive, know, be, and receive that would allow me total clarity and ease with money, prosperity, and abundance?

- Perceive, know, be, and receive what I refuse, dare not, must never, and must also perceive, know, be, and receive that would allow me total clarity and ease with ____. (Whilst this question seems long, each word has been chosen for its energy. The overall effect when this question is asked is to release any unspoken and unrecognized limitations).

Show up as the infinite being you are.
Questions to ask:

- What would I be, if I were being the infinite being I truly am?

- What is it going to take for me to claim and own the capacity to show up as me, the infinite being?

- What are the infinite possibilities for this to happen with ease?

WHAT ELSE IS POSSIBLE?

Throughout this book, we have shared our experience of what it took for us to lead ourselves to success, abundance, prosperity, and money with consciousness. We have provided tools, inspiration, and transformational processes to help you to create prosperity consciousness in your life and to lead yourself to money with consciousness.

We invite you to try these tools for yourself. The ideas we present may sound weird, wacky, and bizarre, but we have discovered for ourselves that they work. By making a deliberate choice to be prosperity conscious, you will set in motion the creation of your own reality and turn your life around.

When abundance is the primary state of your beingness, you will be able to trust something that most others do not trust in themselves. You will be able to trust you. You will trust that there is an abundance of money and resources—a never-ending supply. You will experience a knowing, confidence, gratitude, and certitude that all of your wishes and requirements will be met—and this allows you to act more freely. We are not just talking about money, possessions, and doodads. We are talking about everything—gratitude, success, awareness, knowledge, freedom, power, harmony, fun, and much more. That "knowing and trust" allow you to act more freely. If you do not have the consciousness of abundance, then you will make decisions based on what you want (which is what you lack), not based on what is possible. However, when abundance is the primary state of your beingness, you know everything is possible. How does it get any better than this? What else is possible?

◆　　　◆　　　◆

SELF-INQUIRY WORKBOOK. GETTING TO KNOW YOU! GETTING TO KNOW ALL ABOUT YOU!

Quizzes, Questionnaires, and Practical Processes You Can Use to Lead Yourself to Money with Conscious Awareness

If you are ready to be prosperity consciousness, ready for unbridled joy and an exuberant expression and abundance of life, regardless of life's challenges, then all you have to do is choose consciousness in your life, your work, and everything you do. Each time you choose to expand your prosperity consciousness, you change this world into a place in which people can live with absolute awareness, absolute joy, and absolute abundance. Not just you, but every other being in this world is affected by the choices you make.

Becoming Aware

If your finances are not meeting your needs, then it indicates that you have fixed and limited points of view that are sabotaging your prosperity. The more you become aware of these and consider them as "interesting points of view," the more you can open to manifesting the infinite abundance that is available to you. When you become aware of your points of view about money, you will see that, even when they are not true, they become self-fulfilling if you accept them as true.

As you become aware of how every aspect of your life is being shaped by the unconscious and unexamined points of view you have about money, then your behavior and the way you relate to money will automatically start to shift. Your path to money and prosperity is linked irrevocably to your awareness of your limited points of view. Awareness will set you free.

What is it going to take to ignite and expand your awareness? It is up to you to create your life abundantly and prosperously. Whether you choose a prosperous life or not, we would like you to know that you can.

Everything is a choice.

Everything has infinite possibilities.

Moving Out of the Scarcity Paradigm

To lead yourself to money with consciousness, you must first get yourself out of the scarcity paradigm. Look as clearly and honestly as you can at the paradigm you predominantly utilize to view yourself and the world around you. When you change your focus from scarcity to prosperity consciousness, you can change your financial situation, sometimes instantaneously.

Ask yourself these questions:

1. Do you perceive that you live in an abundant universe?

☐ Yes ☐ No

2. Are you willing to be aware that life is an abundance of everything? Is life an abundance of joy, an abundance of ease, and an abundance of glory? Is this reality the truth of you?

☐ Yes ☐ No

3. Do you perceive that you have the power to choose to operate from prosperity consciousness?

☐ Yes ☐ No

To move out of scarcity and into prosperity, it is essential that you are able to answer "Yes" to all three questions above.

Whether we currently perceive it and know it, or not, we all have the power to choose whether we will live in prosperity consciousness or scarcity consciousness.

What would it take for you to live in the consciousness of abundance and prosperity? Below are some questions that will help you to do three important things:

- Discover the limiting viewpoints out of which you have created your life.

- Recognize how you give away your power and play the victim concerning money.

- Become aware of limiting points of view that keep you from experiencing abundance.

When you answer the questions below, do not write down what you think is the "correct" answer—because there is no such thing. Allow the truth of where you sit to be the answer. Looking at your limitations is not about sitting in judgment of you. It is about becoming aware of how you have created your reality.

1. What is money? What is money to you? (*When you think about money, what are your first thoughts?*)

_____

_____

_____

Money has only the meaning that you assign to it, and you have assigned to it all kinds of meaning and significance. The common answers to the above question are power, mobility, growth, happiness, security, and a cushion for survival.

It's important that you are aware of what your assumptions and definitions of money are, since you're bringing money to yourself with your consciousness. Every point of view that you have about what money is and what it means to you creates the limitations and parameters from which you receive it. For example, if you think that money is power, then when you don't have money, do you feel powerless?

Are you willing to let go of your assumptions and definitions of money?

2. What emotions do you have when you think of money? (*Be honest with yourself. Be honest about what emotion you are feeling. It will do you no good to do this exercise unless you answer truthfully.*)

_____

_____

_____

The emotions you have when you think about money establish how money functions in your life. The common emotions most people have when they think about money are fear, distaste, shame, desire for more, and resistance. One of the most widespread emotions around money is fear that we don't have enough of it, that we always want more.

If you feel that you don't have enough money or if you believe there is not enough to go around, then money can become an obsession for you. It can dominate your thinking, feelings, and actions.

3. What is the financial sob story that you have created as your life? *(What is the story you are telling yourself about your financial situation? What are the assumptions and limiting beliefs you function from in life? These have created your financial destiny and your financial world.)*

Please reflect on how you spend a typical day in conjunction with money. What are you doing and thinking in relation to money? Are you working hard for it, spending it, worrying about not having enough of it, planning what to do with it, or avoiding thinking about it?

Think about these questions the next time you pull out your wallet or checkbook:

- How do you feel when you spend money? Are you functioning from **spending** money or from **creating** money?

- Are you spending from a sense of **loss** or are you **gifting**? Are you spending out of fear, which produces lack, or are you spending with empowerment, which produces more?

Listen to what you are saying to yourself as you hand out money. Listen to your inner voice during your transactions with money. Your attitudes toward money are often indicative of your attitudes toward life itself.

- What is your attitude about gifting? When is it easiest to gift? When is it hardest to gift?

  _____

- Do you gift freely of yourself? Is it hard for you to receive?

  _____

How many assumptions do you have that you are using to create your financial reality and to keep your financial situation limited?

Would you now like to destroy and uncreate everything that creates that situation?

To further clarify this issue, please consider your points of view about your own spending and outflow of money. Tick yes or no for each of the following.

	Yes	No
In general, do you consistently think stressful and negative thoughts about money?		
Do you worry about money when you look at your bank account?		
Do you frequently declare, "I can't afford it"? Do you constantly tell yourself that you are broke or you don't have money to pay for things?		
Do you often give money real supremacy and control over you by infusing it with emotions?		
Do you often worry that you paid too much for something or feel guilty that you bought it?		
Do you end up throwing away your money because you spend it as a way of trying to make yourself happy?		
Do you make choices based on what things cost versus quality and the right fit for you?		

Do you have remorse and guilt about spending money? Do you feel guilty every time you spend money on yourself?

Do you focus more on spending money than on receiving it or having it?

Do you seem to keep creating debt? Do you feel terrible and powerless about the debt you have accrued?

Do you worry about paying for an event that may be happening in the future? Are you concerned about paying bills you expect to receive?

Do you allow money to have power over your life? Do you allow it to become the most important factor in decisions you make about the way you live, work, and play?

Do you use money as a benchmark to evaluate other people or to assess your value, competence, and worth?

If you answered yes to even one of these statements, then you are under the spell of the scarcity mindset. Even one of the above outlooks, deeply ingrained within your psyche, is enough to interfere with your efforts to become wealthy and successful.

These are the thoughts, feelings, and emotions of people who function in the scarcity paradigm. Every time you have these points of view, you are saying, "I lack." If you consistently have these points of view, then you will set yourself up to lack even more. If you start paying attention to what you think and what you judge as right, wrong, good, or bad, then you will see exactly how you are creating the abundance—or the lack of it—that is showing up in your life.

Are you now willing to destroy and uncreate these limiting points of view about money and your financial destiny? If you wish to change your financial situation, then you must destroy and uncreate all of the limiting points of view that you have bought about money and learn to be in allowance of all things.

4. What is your judgment of money?

The following is a list of widespread judgments that can tie you up in personal conflict. See if you identify with them. Put a check next to the ones that you identify with.

- Money is dirty.

- Money is the root of all evil.

- Money is not spiritual.

- Money won't buy you happiness.

- Money doesn't grow on trees.

- Money is scarce.

- Money isn't important.

- Money is a burden.

- Money is a big responsibility.

- Rich people are greedy.

- Rich people aren't like us.

- Rich people don't care about the poor.

- Money causes fighting and unhappiness.

- To make money, I have to have a great job with a high salary.

- There is only so much of the millionaire pie to go around.

- If only I had enough money, then I would be much happier.

- Money is a substitute for love.

- Add your own judgments here:

  _____

  _____

Have you ever had the above points of view about money? If you notice yourself in one of these judgments, then would you like to destroy and uncreate it, please?

The moment you have a judgment about money as bad or wrong or if you see having money as a moral issue, then you stop perceiving and receiving money. Can you see how this works? If you have decided that accumulation of wealth means having more than one's share or gaining at the expense of others, or that wealth ruins the spirit, then you will not be able to perceive or receive any information about how you can create wealth. If you judge that money is dirty, evil, and morally wrong, can you allow yourself to have money? When you have a judgment that money is evil, you won't be able to see the ways in which money can be used to promote life and joy-ousness.

5. How do you describe and portray people with money? What do you think of rich people?

Do you ever feel jealous or resentful of these people? Do you ever mumble, "How come they have money, and I don't"? Do you have judgmental thoughts, feelings, and emotions about them, or do you feel genuinely happy and joyful for them?

_____

_____

What is your first thought when you come face-to-face with obvious illustrations of gargantuan wealth? Anger? Abhorrence? Disapproval? Contempt? Disgust? Jealousy? Distrust? Disrespect? Resentment? Suspicion? Irritation? Does it get on your nerves?

_____

_____

Do you have any bitterness, irritation, anger, or even outright resentment and hostility toward wealthy people?

_____

Do you object to being rich yourself?

_____

Do you have a judgment that rich people have the solution and you don't?

_____

_____

These judgments, thoughts, feelings, and emotions are the major reasons that you have unconsciously repelled money and wealth. It is critical for you to truly perceive this truth. If you view rich people as bad, shameful or disreputable in any way, and you wish to be a good and respectable person, then there is no way you can ever be rich in this lifetime. You cannot possibly allow yourself to be rich. How can you be something you find objectionable and contemptible?

Whenever you catch yourself making judgments or having fixed points of view about money or wealth, just repeat to yourself, "That's an interesting point of view" or "interesting point of view I have this point of view". This statement will release the attachment you have to the energy of that judgment or point of view, and it will free you from it. If you can learn to live from "interesting point of view," you will start to get free of the trauma, drama, upset, and intrigue most people experience in their everyday lives.

Letting Go of Your Scarcity Mindset

If you have scarcity points of view about money, then it is difficult to move through financial limitations, as your points of view unconsciously sabotage your efforts to succeed.

Practical Process: Become aware that most of us buy into the lies and limitations of scarcity. Recognize that no one is kept in poverty due to a deficiency in the supply of wealth. There is enough for everyone. However, to access that truthful experience of *enough*, you have to be willing to relinquish, destroy, and uncreate a lifetime of lies and myths about scarcity. Instead of tormenting yourself about money or choosing a poor quality of life, begin to acknowledge that your apprehensions, uneasiness, and misery about money are not real. When you are able to perceive that they are not real, you will no longer buy into them, and you won't create your life based on what is not real or true.

Would you like to destroy and uncreate any lies about scarcity that you have bought as true? Would you like to destroy and uncreate everything that you have created based on those lies?

You can let go of your scarcity mindset by choosing to let it go. You have to choose to destroy and uncreate the old paradigms and look at the situation anew, through a new lens.

Some of these scarcity points of view may have come into existence because you could not imagine abundance or could not figure out where the money was going to come from. It doesn't matter how you arrived at your limiting points of view. You must destroy and uncreate them. Prosperity begins by perceiving, knowing, being, and receiving the abundance available all around you. Are you willing to perceive, know, be, and receive that you are totally abundant right now?

Ask yourself the following questions:

- Are you willing to give up your no-choice point of view and start recognizing that everything that you are, you have created?

- Are you willing to claim, own, and acknowledge that in one way or another, you have created everything in your life that doesn't work? (This includes relationship problems, work predicaments, physical maladies, pain, discomfort, and financial dilemmas.)

- Are you willing to embrace a new consciousness by acknowledging that the universe consists of unlimited abundance and infinite possibilities?

- Are you willing to give up your fixed points of view about what money has to be or what it has to look like?

- Are you willing to cease resisting and become open to the possibility that there is more to your experience of money than meets the eye?

- Are you willing to perceive, know, be, and receive that abundance is available all around you right now? All the judgments you have set in front of yourself to prevent you from changing your consciousness—can you destroy and uncreate those right now, please?

- Are you getting enjoyment or fulfillment from your work? If not, are you willing to stop only working for the money, out of the belief that this is what's necessary for economic survival? Are you willing to let go of your uncreative, stifling job?

- Are you willing to identify points of view, feelings, and habits that keep you functioning in your scarcity mindset? Are you willing to shift out of resonance with your scarcity paradigm?

- Are you willing to destroy and uncreate the limiting beliefs and points of view that have trapped you in your scarcity paradigm?

When you are willing to let these beliefs go, you will free yourself from your limited patterns of thought, feeling, and behavior. If the answer to any of the questions above is no, or if you are not sure, ask yourself, "What is the value of holding on to this viewpoint?" How much of your awareness do you have to cut off to rigidly hold on to the scarcity paradigm? Would you like to destroy and uncreate all of that, please?

Leading yourself to money with consciousness is about the choices you make. To become prosperous, all you have to do is choose prosperity consciousness. Prosperity consciousness is a choice, as is the scarcity paradigm and anticonsciousness. There is no way to experience joy, bliss, or an exuberant expression of life as long as you are holding on to your scarcity mindset. It's your choice. *Choose!*

What are you not willing to be now, that you would be if you had unlimited amounts of money?

_____

_____

One of the ways to expand your consciousness is to envision and get a sense of what it would be like to be conscious and prosperous. Ask yourself this question: "What would I be if I were being the infinite being I truly am?" If you are going to be conscious and prosperous, who do you have to be? You have to be yourself. You have to claim and own the capacity to show up as you—the infinite being you truly are! You have to be it now, right up front. And you have to destroy

> and uncreate everything that does not allow you to perceive, know, be, and receive who, what, when, where, why, and how you truly are.

Money Is Not the Problem: The Problem Is Our Unwillingness to Receive

The amount of money you have created in your life is in proportion to your willingness to receive it. Your willingness to receive money is conditioned by the point of view you have about how money can flow into your life.

What are you unwilling to receive that would allow more money into your life?

_____

_____

_____

> It is essential to look at what you are unwilling to receive, because this determines the amount of money you are willing to have. The willingness to receive everything is essential if you desire to create wealth. It is also indispensable if you wish to keep it.
>
> A key part of being willing to receive everything is to stop resisting and reacting to any interaction you or anyone else has. When you catch yourself resisting and reacting, ask yourself: What am I unwilling to receive here? What ideas or viewpoints have I created that are stopping me from receiving? What would it be like to receive from everybody without judgment? What would it be like not to have a point of view about _____?

Abundance, prosperity, and wealth are always available to you, but you have to choose to make yourself available to them. Are you willing to receive, claim, own, and acknowledge that you are worthy of abundance, prosperity, and wealth?

The questions that you must ask yourself are: Do I have a sincere aspiration and willingness to have communion with money? Am I willing to be prosperous now?

The answer can only be yes or no, because wishful desire does not provide the fertile inner ecology required for consciousness to expand.

Key Points to Lead Yourself to Money with Conscious Awareness

- True abundance has nothing to do with what you *have*. It has everything to do with who you choose to *be*.

- The universe is an abundant place. There are truly infinite possibilities.

- If you choose to be prosperous and to be prosperity consciousness, then you can be. If you choose to be unconscious and to live in the scarcity paradigm, then you create your life based on that. It's your choice!

- Your consciousness always determines your conditions and circumstances. Unless your prosperity consciousness expands, your relationship with money will remain the same. You will have the same degree of limitation and the same degree of financial mess.

- The key to transforming your consciousness around money is to take a leadership role in your life. You must choose to become the leader of your own life and the creator of your own reality. You must begin to expand your ability to receive everything with gratitude and without judgment.

- To embrace prosperity consciousness, you have to step up and become more than you have been willing to be. This means you must become willing to be more in every respect. You have to stop refusing to be everything you truly are. Are you willing to step out of the scarcity paradigm and become the outstanding, glorious, and magnificent being you truly are?

- Money is actually easy to attract. There is an abundance of money and resources, a never ending supply. It is only your unwillingness to receive that makes money hard for you to obtain.

- Your ability to create unlimited amounts of money is conditioned by two factors: the point of view you have about money and your resistance to it. These are the factors that create your unwillingness to receive.

- The main thing you are unwilling to receive is the greatness of you. If you are willing to receive the uniqueness and the greatness of you, and if you are willing to allow the world and everyone to see the uniqueness and the greatness of you, then the world will gift to you what you truly deserve.

- When you receive the greatness you truly are, then everything in your life will start to transform—including your financial situation. Being open and willing to receive everything with gratitude and without judgment will allow you to expand your awareness and ability and to access infinite possibilities.

- All of your unwillingness to receive the greatness of who you truly are, and all of the talents, abilities, and awareness that you decided you couldn't have—will you now claim, own, and acknowledge them and destroy and uncreate everything that doesn't allow them to exist?

FURTHER READING

If you would like more in-depth information about the tools presented in this book, then the following are recommended reading materials.

Conscious Leadership: The Key to Unlocking Success
By Chutisa Bowman and Steven Bowman, with major contributions by Gary Douglas

Magic. You ARE It. BE it.
By Gary M. Douglas and Dr. Dain C. Heer

Money Isn't the Problem, You Are
By Gary M. Douglas and Dr. Dain C. Heer

Sex Is Not a Four Letter Word but Relationship Often Times Is
By Gary M. Douglas and Dr. Dain C. Heer

Embodiment
The manual you should have been given when you were born
By Dr. Dain C. Heer

For more information on these books, go to www.accessconsciousness.com

ABOUT THE AUTHORS

Chutisa Bowman

Chutisa is a director and cofounder of LifeMastery, based in Melbourne, Australia. She has embraced a career as an international adviser and facilitator in the field of transpersonal counseling, ergonomics, behavioral self-management, and stress intervention. Formerly a senior executive at a number of Australia's largest publicly listed retail corporations, and a senior consultant with one of Australia's most prominent usability and human factors specialist consulting firms, Chutisa perceives and knows from firsthand experience what businesses and leaders need to do to become more effective and conscious. Concurrent with her ability in assisting individuals and organizations attain improved efficiency and wakefulness, Chutisa has insight into the challenges and opportunities of integrating consciousness into a business environment. She has been focusing on developing processes to help companies build a culture of consciousness and conscious leadership teams, and on helping people deal with everyday stress in demanding environments. Chutisa uses her own experience and many years of research to help today's leaders, managers, and employees expand their consciousness and change the culture of their workplaces.

Trained as both a transpersonal and conventional psychophysical change facilitator, Chutisa received her undergraduate qualification from the IKON Institute in transpersonal counseling, her post-graduate degree from La Trobe University, Melbourne, Australia, in Ergonomics/Human Factors, and a master's degree in counseling from Monash University, Melbourne, Australia. She has gone beyond her traditional academic training, however, by acquiring a depth and breadth of knowledge in a number of fields, including ACCESS Energy for Transformation, behavioral medicine, stress and well-being, HeartMath processes, and meditation. She has also extensively studied consciousness, creativity, and the great spiritual traditions of the world.

◆   ◆   ◆

Steven Bowman

Steven Bowman is a director and cofounder of LifeMastery, based in Melbourne, Australia. He is sought after by businesses around the world as an expert adviser on conscious leadership, strategic innovation, and awakening the power of consciousness within organizations. Steve is one of Australia's leading governance and senior executive team specialists, having previously held positions as national executive director of the Australasian Institute of Banking and Finance, CEO of the Finance and Treasury Association, general manager of ExpoHire (Australia) Pty Ltd, assistant director of the Australian Society of CPAs, and director of the American College of Health Care Administrators. He is a past president of the Australian Society of Association Executives and has held numerous other board positions.

Steve has authored and coauthored over fourteen books on governance and executive leadership. He was the founder and associate program director of the certificate and advanced certificate in association management at Monash Mt Eliza Business School for eleven years. He and his partner, Chutisa, currently consult with over one thousand not-for-profit and corporate organizations each year in Australia, New Zealand, USA, and Asia.

Steve is a warm and engaging conference keynote speaker and dynamic workshop/seminar facilitator. He brings thirty years of hands-on experience and delivers it in a down-to-earth style that speaks to everyone throughout an organization. He leaves his audiences inspired, with practical leadership tools and tips that they can apply at work, at home, and in their communities.

Trained in both organizational management and as a behavioral scientist, Steve received his undergraduate degree in applied science, speech pathology, from La Trobe University, where he also completed a post-graduate degree in communication disorders. He completed his master's degree from George Washington University, Washington DC, in speech pathology, where he also completed a master's degree in association management. He also earned a certificate in association management and an advanced certificate in association management at the Mt. Eliza Business School.

◆   ◆   ◆

Gary Douglas

Gary Douglas is a director and founder of Access Energy for Transformation, based in Santa Barbara, California. During his forty years in business, he has been a director, manager, entrepreneur, and business owner in areas as diverse as real estate, restaurant management, horse training, and antiques. Gary is widely recognized as a leader in the field of consciousness and energy transformation process. He is one of the world's foremost catalysts in helping individuals to claim, own, and acknowledge their ability to perceive, know, be, and receive their true greatness. He is continually focused on assisting people to reach greater freedom, consciousness, and awareness of their talents, abilities, and capabilities.

Gary used his own methods and processes to create his dream job and lifestyle. He currently travels throughout the world, consulting with individuals and groups and guiding them to personal freedom. A convivial, affable, and powerful presenter, Gary invites his listeners to empower their bodies, hearts, and psyches, and expand their consciousness and transform their lives.

◆   ◆   ◆

MORE ABOUT LIFEMASTERY

LifeMastery is an international organization dedicated to facilitating individual and organizational transformation. Its goal is to expand consciousness in the workplace so that consciousness can spread throughout society and transform the world.

LifeMastery's founders, Steve and Chutisa Bowman, have worked with presidents, CEOs, and senior leaders, to bring about dramatic organizational improvements in the fields of health, trade, employment, finance, sports, telecommunications, religion, higher education, philanthropy, and welfare, as well as in not-for-profit and community organizations. LifeMastery's conscious leadership development programs support CEOs and their teams in developing conscious partnerships with their boards. LifeMastery's programs achieve sustainable results by aligning leadership teams and staff with organizational vision and strategies and by creating synchronization and harmony between executives, leadership teams, staff, and stakeholders.

LifeMastery is breaking new ground in therapeutic processes for leading organizational transformation. LifeMastery provides a practical framework and comprehensive approach to help businesses expand and enhance their consciousness levels, facilitating magnification of consciousness in governance and empowering directorships of boards of commercial, public, and not-for profit-organizations. LifeMastery is dedicated to inspiring individuals and organizations to expand their consciousness and fulfill their potentials. The founders of LifeMastery believe that the best way to achieve expansion of the world is through the facilitation of consciousness in all things.

LifeMastery has a proven track record of infusing leaders, teams, and individuals with enthusiasm and excitement, creating a culture in which people can find balance and become highly conscious, and emphasizing not just professional and financial rewards but also the psychological, emotional, and intellectual rewards of a job well done.

For more information about LifeMastery and
Steven and Chutisa Bowman, visit www.lifemastery.com.au.

MORE ABOUT ACCESS ENERGY FOR TRANSFORMATION

Access Energy for Transformation is an applied philosophy for living that has been successfully put into practice by individuals all over the world for expansion of their lives. Access empowers people to become conscious of and to shift any areas of their lives that aren't working. This includes the common, everyday things people have trouble with, such as financial dilemmas; relationship problems; career obstacles; lack of pleasure, satisfaction, ease, or bliss in life; uncertainty about the purpose and impetus of life; and the inability to achieve what they know they are capable of.

Access also deals with and brings clarity to some of the strange, unexplained, or weird experiences that people have. This can include the phenomena of hearing voices in one's head, or becoming anxious, depressed, sick, or having physical problems when the people around one are being these. Access works on just about any difficulty and produces the possibility for a change in all aspects of life.

Access Energy for Transformation helps individuals to embrace a place of infinite possibilities that resides within each of us. Access Energy provides a set of tools and processes designed to create freedom from the limitations of the past. It enables a person to create a life full of ease, joy, glory, and constant wonderful surprises. Access tools and processes allow people to remove the limitations that shackle and chain them, so they can shift what isn't working and step into *beingness* and the *magic* of life!

Access is a gentle way to remove energy blockages and to unlock everything that does not allow people to be everything they would like to be, or to have everything they would like to have. Clearing these energy blockages allows the body, mind, and spirit to align as Oneness. This creates dramatic changes in people's interactions with others and in the productivity of their lives. Access began in 1990, based on information that Gary Douglas channeled, and he has been developing and refining it ever since. Access uses both verbal clearing processes and simple, but phenomenally powerful, hands-on healing techniques to create increased consciousness. Most of the people who have attended Access workshops have discovered a new sense of what their potential is, how to unlock it, and how to access it. The techniques work on adults, children, and animals.

The information presented in this book is actually just a small taste of what Access has to offer. There is a whole universe of Access processes and classes. If there are places where you can't get things to work in your life the way you know they ought to, then you might like to attend Access classes. For more information about Access Energy for Transformation and Gary Douglas, visit this Web site:

www.accessconsciousness.com

MORE INFORMATION ON
RESOURCES

Are you interested in having one of the authors work with your organization or your leadership team? To find out about our availability, contact us:

Steven and Chutisa Bowman
LifeMastery (Aust) PTY LTD
Phone 61 3 9509 9529
or email bowman@lifemastery.com.au
www.the2bowmans.com

Gary Douglas
Access Energy for Transformation
Phone 1 805 331 8413
or email info@accessconsciousness.com

Gary Douglas and Steven and Chutisa Bowman
also provide on-site conscious leadership or prosperity creation retreats and developmental programs for organizations both domestically and internationally. Please check the Web sites for more details.

LifeMastery (Aust) Pty Ltd
www.lifemastery.com.au

Access Energy for Transformation
www.accessconsciousness.com

978-0-595-42596-9
0-595-42596-8

17862581R00095

Made in the USA
Lexington, KY
06 October 2012